TURNING 50

TURNING 50

Fifty Personal Celebrations

OLIVIA WU

**Andrews McMeel
Publishing**

Kansas City

to Simon

00 01 02 03 04 RDC 10 9 8 7 6 5 4 3 2 1

Library of Congress Cataloging-in-Publication Data

Wu, Olivia, columnist.
    Turning 50 : fifty personal celebrations / Olivia Wu.
        p. cm.
    ISBN 0-7407-0054-5
    1. Middle-aged persons—United States—Anniversaries, etc. 2. Birthdays—United States. 3. Middle age—United States—Psychological aspects. I. Title. II. Title: Turning fifty.
HQ1059.5.U5W8 2000
305.244—dc21   99-41932
                                                            CIP

Book design by Holly Camerlinck

——— ATTENTION: SCHOOLS AND BUSINESSES ———

Andrews McMeel books are available at quantity discounts with bulk purchase for educational, business, or sales promotional use. For information, please write to: Special Sales Department, Andrews McMeel Publishing, 4520 Main Street, Kansas City, Missouri 64111.

Contents

VIII Adventure

IX Power

X Purpose

XI Community

CONTENTS

PREFACE

When I walked out of the ballet for Joe Schuman's birthday, I was struck by the combination of generosity, humor, and creativity—the *grace*—with which he had put together his birthday celebration. Here was someone of my generation who emerged from the last thirty years with values intact, personality intact, and yet somehow also radically transformed. Here he was, showing self-love with wisdom and wit. Here he was, using the resources of middle age to express the modified dreams and ideology of youth, now softened with compassion, humility, and a twinkle in his eye.

Indeed, it was something to celebrate.

It occurred to me that Joe's buying of the balcony for a ballet performance by a struggling troupe and his diverting the would-be gifts from four hundred guests into the causes he supports could not be a lone act. There *had* to be other baby boomers, who, having gone through the fire, had come out still giving, still living their consciences, still creative, and still bucking tradition. Still full of life.

We were in middle age, but surely we were not all bowing to the conventions of the black balloons and comedic and real angst? We were still ourselves although we were transformed. We, who had written our own marriage vows and created rituals for our children's births, and were now opening the discussion on menopause—we would be undoing old rituals, resurrecting and creating others for this passage. How, indeed, did we pull what we did in the '60s and '70s into the '90s?

I began to look. I found plenty about midlife crises, including on the Internet. Mike Bellah, author and columnist, maintains a Web site called "Our Best Years" (www.bestyears.com), which receives two thousand hits a day. On it, one can access a list of his columns, one of which is "Turning 40, Turning 50." He tunes into the angst of this generation. Crisis may be too strong a word, he says, but this is certainly a generation that expected too much and therefore failed. "We grew up in a really unique time in United States history. Parents who grew up in the

Depression were raising children in the country's most affluent time and reiterated the message of how lucky they were. "What they failed to tell us is life is tough. We were totally unprepared for that," Bellah said.

One of the products of a childhood lived in comfort was altruism. The Vietnam War, however, changed that. "All the altruism hit the '70s and died for most people." There followed a driven quality in our lives, a quest for self-fulfillment. The result was, "no one became all that they wanted to be."

Yet Joe Schuman, having let go of some ideals and expectations, made peace, and indeed found happiness, and became what he wanted to be as he was discovering what he wanted to be. I was certain there were many others.

I found them—especially women. Many knew they were extending the biological and social markers of their age by raising toddlers, either adopting them or even giving birth to them. Menopause liberated many; having grown children liberated even more. Others felt the intense intimacy of life and death in the day-by-day care of aging or dying parents. Some had survived bouts with cancer.

Celebration and ritual can mark a milestone, but they can in themselves be transformative. They are a public, outer acknowledgment of inner achievements and they can bless new intentions. Having marked a stage with ritual, one can move forward, or having recognized a happening as seminal, one can acknowledge it formally. This book is the story of such celebrations by "ordinary" people who recognized something extraordinary in themselves and about the lives they were living.

ACKNOWLEDGMENTS

This book is about ties. By age fifty, we have many ties and the wisdom to acknowledge their surprising roles and incalculable worth in the web of living. Of the fifty or so subjects in this book, everyone is in some way connected to me through personal ties, sometimes twice or three times removed. I happened upon only a handful that I can say were truly strangers. My thanks, then, do not and cannot trace all the interweavings of this ethereal web. Suffice it to say this book simply would not exist without the unique individuals who entered my life by the intricate and sometimes mysterious connections of life.

To Glen Tig, Deann Bayless, Peg Tappe, Bev Bennett, and Jan Steinmark I give thanks for their big hearts, which remember the big events of their big list of friends. I thank

Roger Ebert for telling me I could write and for giving me the benefit of his publishing experience. I thank Rhea Dawson and especially Simon Noël for helping me through the stages of producing a manuscript. I thank all those I consider my extended family for nurturing me and sustaining me through the dream. I am grateful to my former editor, Donna Martin, for seeing the potential in this project. Finally, I thank Patricia Rice, my editor, for her openness, enthusiasm, and passionate friendship with all the subjects in the book, none of whom she met but all of whom she embraced.

Introduction

DEEPAK CHOPRA:
THOUGHTS ON AGING

I did not mark fifty. It doesn't mean anything," he said.

I had been certain Deepak Chopra, mind-body guru, author, physician, scientist, philosopher, and poet, would speak words of inspired wisdom and encouragement on the subject of turning fifty. He would have a creative response to the question, "How did you celebrate fifty?"

Instead, he was erasing the idea of chronological age itself. "People ask me what does it feel like to be middle-aged and I say, 'I'll tell you when I get there.'"

Chopra, who by conventional accounting turned fifty in 1996, rises at 4 A.M. and works through to 10 P.M. daily. At his Chopra Center for Wellness in La Jolla, California, he writes, consults, sees patients, meets with staff, leads them in meditation, works out, meditates alone, and draws from a well of energy that belongs to a youthful person. "I feel the same as I felt when I was twenty. Emotionally I feel a little more mature but I feel the same enthusiasm and wonder for my life as I felt then."

In denying the marker of biological and chronological age, he made of turning fifty simultaneously a nonevent as well as a wondrous time of life. While he was eliminating the basis of my central question, he was speaking to the core issue of living and aging.

He began to describe those qualities that transcend time and age. These emotions and experiences, he said, lend meaning to life and exist beyond the boundaries of real time and common experience: love, joy, gratitude, creativity, compassion, dreams, and purpose.

Love, joy, gratitude, creativity, compassion, dreams, purpose—I was astonished. These were the very feelings to which the people in my book gave voice. He was echoing, with powerful words and ideas, those very realities that they had discovered.

"I don't really think in terms of how old people are other than I find people who are chronologically, biologically, or emotionally very old." Youthfulness exists beyond biological age, he said. "The experience of youth is totally dependent on whether you feel connected to the source of creation itself. Do you feel a sense of joy all the time and do you have the ability to spread it to others? Does your life have a sense of meaning? A sense of compassion? If you have all the above you have a lot to do. There's no time to worry about aging."

© Jeremiah Sullivan 1999

Middle age is a social perception, and "human aging is not a fixed phenomenon. It is even reversible. Throughout history, those who were "old" gifted civilization with incalculable riches. He listed [George Bernard] Shaw, Tolstoy, Churchill, Picasso, and Michaelangelo as among those from whom civilizations benefited when they were in their eighties and nineties.

The generation of Americans turning fifty, the baby boomers, holds a powerful promise, he said. "For the first time we are going to see a critical mass of people that can completely change the world. We should start saying it's glamorous to be older. When we start venerating the elderly, giving them more respect and responsibility, and when we start recognizing that they have the wisdom of experience, that will happen." This generation also has the benefit of scientific research on biology and youth to extend its vigor. Experiments with eighty- and ninety-year-olds have shown that if they are put through a conditioning program, they can become healthier and more vital than those who are fifty and sixty. With breath and weight training, sensory stimulation, and meditation—which changes the internal attitudes—they can "actually reverse the bio-markers of aging," he said.

Body fat content, aerobic ability, cholesterol (HDL–LDL ratio), sexual drive, hearing, and blood sugar content are among those markers that "are all completely reversible."

Many cultural models embrace aging rather than deny

it. Some are enlightened. "In my [Indian]Vedic tradition, fifty is your second birth. It is time to wake up the gods and goddesses in your psyche." In every woman are the goddesses Hera, Athena, Aphrodite, Persephone, Artemis, and Demeter. By summoning Aphrodite, the goddess of love, for example, a woman frees herself to experience sensuality and sexuality. Similarly, Demeter, the goddess of agriculture, can channel "the life energy and fertility of the mother into creativity because she's done with biological creativity."

In the Vedic tradition, from age fifty to age seventy-five is the time of wisdom and transformation, he said. "You change your attention from family to society at large. At the same time, it is a personal journey of transformation where you go from ordinary states of consciousness to higher states. You are waking to glimpse soul.

"This is the time to start to wake up."

He himself is a prime example. "I personally feel younger than I did twenty-five years ago, when I was smoking and doing other [nonhealthful] things. My creativity and physical output are more. My father is eighty and I can't keep up with him. He is making plans for ten years from now. He has no time to think about aging."

It turns out that Chopra does mark his birthdays. "I go into silence for that week." As he does several times a year, he retreats into complete privacy. In solitude, he performs his personal rituals.

Rituals are important to living fully and wholly, he said. And rituals or ceremonies, which many of the subjects in this book created, serve a purpose. "Ritual is a way of trapping intention and attention. It is a profound thing to do. It gives meaning to something which inherently may not have had meaning," he said. "It helps one pay attention to the intuitive, visionary, sacred, creative response."

Ritual includes celebration. "Celebration is a ritual that acknowledges gratitude, transformation, transition, so traditionally we've celebrated bar mitzvahs, birthdays. . . . We celebrate every transition of life."

Ritual, celebration, gratitude, transformation, transition, life, death—these surrounded the experiences and insights that nearly everyone in this book captured. The most universal was gratitude. A profound thankfulness beats in the hearts of every subject in this book. For most, it led to a spiritual opening. "Gratitude is one of the best ways to get in touch with your soul," Chopra said.

Knowing this, the challenge at fifty is apparent. "Start thinking 'What can I do for the world' and get busy doing it. Nelson Mandela and Mother Teresa weren't worried about themselves." To do that, "You must take care of yourself. It's best to be totally vital in the present with nutrition, nutritional supplements, exercise, meditation, stress management, and changing internal attitudes.

"Have a dream, make your life worthwhile. If you touch people and you are fulfilled that way, you'll have more."

Gratitude gives birth to transformation. "Nothing ever comes to an end, it only transforms," he said. At the same time, an awareness of death infuses every transformation with greater consciousness.

"If you are aware that the Prince of Death is stalking you, that every minute he's closer, your life would be totally magical. Your priorities wouldn't be trivial—they would be magnificent things."

1 Sunrise

A Ritual for Rebirth

DONALD SKINNER

unrise signifies beginnings for Don Skinner, so on May 16, 1996, he took fifteen friends to a hilltop near his home at 5:55 A.M. for a short ceremony. It was how he wanted to mark his fiftieth birthday. "Throughout my life I have often sought out the very beginnings of the day to give me inspiration for the hours and the questions that followed . . ." he would say to them.

In most work-a-day lives, sunrise is witnessed alone, if at all. To share it with others is rare.

"I wanted something people should make a little more effort to get to," he said. Initially, "I wanted something all my friends could share and something more than a party with food and drink." Then, it all came to him—to gather friends and family with a ceremony and in surroundings

2

that have always held meaning. "Nature is a big part of my life and I wanted to be outside."

In ritual he could assemble words, symbols, and gestures and create out of them a formal marking of this passage. Like many of his generation, he had discarded worn ceremonies and sought new ones. For his wedding he and his wife used a ceremony written by a friend. "As I have aged, I've become more emotional and perhaps more open to ritual . . . also with age comes a desire to make your life count for something, to figure out what's important. So that's in there, too."

In midlife, he is grateful for those customs of his childhood that have fed his attraction to ritual: the vivid poetry of Protestant hymns ("fountains filled with blood and ties that bind"), the memory of his father picking the first rose of summer for his mother and the family reunions on a midwestern farm. Living on a farm blessed him with a great gift, the two daily markers of sunrise and sunset.

His own family now marks the winter solstice with a gathering of friends, a candle ceremony, and a recounting of things to let go and things to be grateful for. He also draws inspiration from the Unitarian Universalist Church, where he receives "the encouragement to find your own spiritual path and to develop personal rituals that are meaningful."

Skinner, a former journalist and now a freelance writer, wrote his invitation as well as the ceremony, which he called a "Fiftieth Birthday Commemoration Ritual." They are both informed by quiet grace and wry humor, rather like the way he speaks. He wanted his friends to get up early, but he also pre-forgave them with this footnote: "The morning event should not be construed as a test of friendship."

In the end, "all the people who mattered showed up." They found themselves participating in a thoughtful twenty-minute ritual of readings, responses, chime ringing, and symbolic acts that moved them deeply.

With levity-laced solemnity, the fifteen hiked up to a hill in suburban Kansas City. There, Don welcomed them to the beautiful sunrise and struck the bronze circles of two Tibetan cymbals. As the pure, high tone rang, it rippled in the morning air. It seemed to vibrate infinitely. "I ring a chime for the morning of the first day of the fiftieth year of my life. For half a century now the sun has come up on a world in which I have been a part," he began.

There followed readings and responses, including passages from Henry David Thoreau's essay "To Live Deliberately." The Tibetan chime's ethereal tone separated the sections.

The heart of the ceremony pertained to letting go, to welcoming freedom, to emphasizing what is important. "Turning fifty means that you're letting go of some dreams that might have been possible when you were younger but probably aren't now, like you might not climb that mountain. It also means freedom in that you don't have to climb that mountain."

He read, "Being fifty means I am free from having to change the world, but not free from having to try . . . I do not have to be all things to all people . . . It is a time to learn new skills, to pick up the harmonica and the saxophone and the soccer ball. It is time to treat my time and my self well . . ."

In the second part of the ceremony, he acknowledged the importance of the community of friends. "Friendship binds us together. We celebrate our relationship, one to another, and remember the good times we have had and the good times which are to come—as long as there aren't any more stupid sunrise ceremonies."

In the third part of the ritual, he recognized birth:

5

TURNING FIFTY MEANS
THAT YOU'RE LETTING
GO OF SOME DREAMS
THAT MIGHT HAVE BEEN
POSSIBLE WHEN YOU
WERE YOUNGER BUT
PROBABLY AREN'T NOW,
LIKE YOU MIGHT NOT
CLIMB THAT MOUNTAIN.
IT ALSO MEANS
FREEDOM IN THAT YOU
DON'T HAVE TO CLIMB
THAT MOUNTAIN.
—*Don Skinner*

"New opportunities rise before me at this milestone and I pray that I am equal to them . . . From this point on I am going to be a slightly different person. I shall wear more purple, be less inhibited, write more letters to public officials, wear shoes without socks, and signal my turns earlier . . ."

He closed the ceremony with the human and the infinitely small to express infinity. "There have been many memorable moments in fifty years. I may have measured out my life in coffee spoons, but I have also measured it in beach sand and mountain meadows, in work that I cared about and in rewarding human relationships and the creativity of my hands and mind and in the sharing of myself in a multitude of ways . . .

"And I am richer for all of those . . ."

Then he released a helium balloon. To the balloon were attached notes from each participant. "We wrote messages about things we wanted to release from our lives." It was "a chance to think about what you might like to change in your own life and send it aloft and away."

In silence, but with the echo of the Tibetan chimes in their inner ears, "we watched it float away from the city."

11 Integration

Graduation

ANN WATERS

SEPTEMBER 9, 1947

The summer before she turned fifty, Ann Waters earned a master's degree. Then she sea-kayaked with Outward Bound. They seemed appropriate ways to mark the milestone.

"Fifty is such a round number and a number we all spend a good amount of time fearing," she said. "Here I was turning fifty, which seemed old, but I was starting on a new job. That seemed to buffer the old middle-agedness of fifty."

Her unrest had simmered after she attended her college reunion in 1994. "At the twenty-fifth reunion, it was asked, have you followed your basic values? You can't help but look at what you've done and you ask, 'Is it worthwhile?'" Then, there's "the old burden, 'Could I have done it better?' No, don't go there."

She didn't, but she did take stock, however, drew conclusions, and acted. "There's a sense you've made your choices and you can't go back on them. I did all those things, which means I didn't do other things, and it's time to take stock."

She decided that twenty-plus years of freelance editing ("it was all good" for herself and her three children) were wearing. Even taking up piano was not working. Both involved "intense mental efforts with me sitting alone."

She researched careers and degrees. During this time, death dogged her. Both her father and father-in-law died, and as she started her program, her mother died also. Those events fueled her progress. "My education had been important to my parents, and I know that I was thinking of them throughout my studies." She began a degree in speech language pathology, related to, but quite different from her English major.

Being an older graduate student gave her multiple perspectives. First, unlike undergraduate school, "I really enjoyed grad school and working hard on something I cared about." As much as the memories of her parents spurred her, it was the other sandwiching generation that provided a different perspective and delight. All three teenagers "were sort of glad that I was so busy that I couldn't interfere with them." And "My working so much gave me a new appreciation of the stresses and demands on their lives in school, and a new and healthy sense of their separate identities."

Details of new studenthood fed her sense of humor. "I got a new backpack to use as a book bag, which my kids thought was pretty funny, after having picked out so many new book bags for them over the years."

Especially, "they enjoyed watching how interested I was in listening for school cancellations on snowy days."

She also gained perspective about her work when she compared herself and her contemporaries to those classmates who were freshly graduated from college. "The ones who were older had an easier time and weren't worried about the schoolness of it."

She befriended many in their thirties who were restarting careers. She was more like them: "People who had career goals just focused on what they had learned." Yet, she cut a different edge. "I love being able to say I haven't done that for thirty years." She didn't feel matronly, just different and glad to be so.

To top off her celebratory year, she signed up for a

week-long, Outward Bound, sea-kayaking trip. "Partly, I felt I needed to keep this growth curve. I also felt capable of doing new things. Outward Bound pushes you to trust yourself and trust the people you're with."

In the face of her parents dying and her children leaving the nest, "I felt I needed to strengthen myself, literally and spiritually." She was creating a new self. "Who was I? What was I going to do next? It seemed like a new era in my life that I needed to get ready for—who knows for what?"

I DON'T FEEL MATRONLY, BUT I MADE FRIENDS WHO WERE THIRTY YEARS OLD, AND I LOVE BEING ABLE TO SAY I HAVEN'T DONE THAT FOR THIRTY YEARS.

—Ann Waters

13

JOE SCHUMAN

DECEMBER 3, 1946

In the fall of 1996, some four hundred of Joe Schuman's friends received an invitation to the dance. He couldn't think of a better way to celebrate his fiftieth birthday than by spending an afternoon surrounded by his friends at a ballet. He wrote on the invitation: "I expect to share a first-class performance of a piece I treasure with a balcony full of people whom I treasure more."

The Chicago lawyer created an event that embraced all parts of his life. The gathering of family, friends, and clients to share a longtime passion was the natural expression of a man who has sought wholeness and supported high causes all his life—including knowing a good deal when he saw one.

The invitation itself conveyed the magnitude of a wedding and the simplicity of a memorial. It was simultaneously grandiose and intimate. Like Joe, it was lawyerly and airtight in design but childlike and whimsical in tone. It included:

1. RSVP cards that read "Dear Joe, We may not like you much but if you're paying, we're coming. Please send _____ tickets to _____";

2. Synopsis of the ballet;

3. Map to the theater;

4. "Joe's Ballet Pantomime 101," a preperformance talk on ballet language; and

5. Gift directions. (*Absolutely no presents please.* If, in your heart, you want to do something, please consider sharing some time or money with one of these organizations.")

There were three options under gifts: "In the aesthetic mode, Ballet Theater of Chicago; in the political mode, Venceremos Brigade; in the spiritual mode, the Buddhist Society for Compassionate Wisdom." (Venceremos Brigade is an organization of pro-Cuba activists who support Castro and the revolution. The Buddhist Society for Compassionate Wisdom is Joe's local temple.)

This overture framed a Sunday afternoon performance of *Giselle* by the then-fledgling Ballet Theater of Chicago. BTC, like other start-up ballet companies, danced before skimpy houses and operated a foreshortened season of about ten weeks. That Sunday afternoon, BTC danced to a nearly full balcony.

Joe arrived at the theater on foot (he does not own a car), his thinning, implanted hair disheveled, a child of the '60s in the body of an avuncular patron. He surveyed the balcony with wonder. His eyes twinkled. Buddhists, pro-Cuba activists, and octogenarian Jewish relatives were rubbing shoulders. He grinned. "Holy shit," the eyes shouted behind his glasses.

The inspiration for the event grew out of contentment. "I was feeling good about fifty. I continue to feel that the things that I've lost are more than made up for by the things I've gained. I feel very much at peace. I had let go of saving the world, I had let go of becoming a household word, I had let go of being physically attractive. I was able to just be."

Just being permitted spontaneity.

He had gone to BTC's performance of *Giselle* the year before to show support and expected little. "Instead, I discovered the troupe was wonderful," he said. "They were not sold out and tickets were dirt cheap. I was thinking how much they would ask for the whole balcony. Well, I called and they gave me a price. I couldn't turn it down!" he said, sheepish and victorious.

Then began a process of planning and mailings that delighted him more than the event itself. He culled the invitation list from his meticulous, twenty-five-year-old family-client list.

Dance was drummed into the rhythm of Joe's life from childhood. He studied tap dance through high school. In college he was a member of a performing folk dance troupe. As a law student at the University of

I CONTINUE TO FEEL THAT THE THINGS THAT I'VE LOST ARE MORE THAN MADE UP FOR BY THE THINGS I'VE GAINED.

—*Joe Schuman*

Chicago, "My major luxury was gallery seats at the Auditorium Theater for the dance series." Yet the memory of movement still lives in his cells, something he says that cannot "be responded to verbally."

He does respond verbally about his lifelong dance with socialism, which has led him in a pas de deux of complex turns. Now the drama seems to rest in a state of graceful compassion. It was not always so.

With blueblood academic genes, he was guaranteed a place in his father's law firm. However, his social conscience dictated otherwise. Having served as a conscientious objector and counseled draft resistors after college, he entered law school with the aim of becoming a "people's revolutionary lawyer."

Instead, he discovered he was happiest when he pointed his career on a quiet and solo course, as an estate lawyer. "This practice is good for me. I don't have to kick people. I can do [wills] for them, and get them more than they thought. I'm very custodial, very pastoral about my clients. I work from a script of earning and redeeming trust."

Modesty is a theme. He lives on fifty-thousand-dollar annual net earnings, which does feed his habit when the three-month dance season arrives in town.

When American Ballet Theatre failed to tour Chicago in 1995 he went to Russia for one week of the Kirov Ballet. There, in the aftermath of communism, he witnessed the transition of Marxism to capitalism. Marxism had failed but capitalism was looking hellishly ugly. The grim consequences of both capitalism and communism depressed him.

It was Buddhism that entered the dance and introduced grace. Buddhism pointed to inner choices. "Buddhism means we don't have to live this way. Even as the world goes to hell in a hand basket, I can still be okay."

He had impishly seated the Buddhists next to the pro-Cuba activists at the ballet and he relished the irony, but the two sides of him now coexist in enlightened social consciousness. He regularly attends his temple, occasionally lecturing there, he writes a column about homosexuals, and he encourages whomever he meets to go to Cuba.

He discovered Cuba shortly after his Russia trip. "Cuba was practically a conversion experience. I am now feeling less pessimistic for the human race than I have in thirty years." Cuba represented the social equivalent of not going to hell in a hand basket, just as Buddhism represented a personal salvation from a world spinning out of control.

JOSEPH
SCHUMAN
ATTORNEY

November 17, 1996

Dear Friends,

Please help me celebrate my fiftieth birthday by joining me as my guest to see Ballet Theatre of Chicago dance <u>Giselle</u> at 1:00 on Saturday, March 22, at the Athenaeum Theatre, 2936 N. Southport.

Our seats aren't in the Czar's private box. You'll need to climb stairs and may want to bring a seat cushion. But I expect to share a first-class performance of a piece I treasure with a balcony full of people whom I treasure more.

Cordially,

P.S. I've promised to release seats I don't use, so please return the enclosed card by December 15.

208 SOUTH
LASALLE
SUITE 725
CHICAGO
ILLINOIS
60604

(312)
701-0400

There's nothing magical about the number fifty, however. If he'd had the same peace at age forty-five, it would have felt good then. Whenever it happens, it is a result of "accumulated mistakes and the hormones quieting down." He falls back on the language of Buddhism to express being fifty: "It is a place where I feel I have found balance."

A Day for Women

DAYLE HADDON

MAY 26, 1948

Supermodel Dayle Haddon celebrated fifty by spending the entire day with the people who support her most, her women friends.

"A girlfriend is more important than a therapist and a husband. A girlfriend comes through in the difficult times and in great times. The complicity of a girlfriend is so full because [the relationship] is for life."

Her day began with a breakfast for three, progressed to a surprise luncheon for eight, dinner for six, and segued into dancing at the Rainbow Room in New York City.

"It was a love day—a day of laughter," was how she summed it up. Her friends knew she loved surprises and each meal was one in a series of surprises. The arrangement was perfect for her because "I love surprise celebra-

22

tions. I love my birthdays. I tell people months ahead about my birthday." As for her fiftieth, "I told people for the last five years" that I was turning fifty.

"It's an honor."

Honor built itself brick by brick for this model who persisted in knocking on fashion's door for ten years until she succeeded. She was cover material in European magazines and only slowly did she catch on in the United States. Eventually, she shared covers with the likes of Lauren Hutton.

None of this happened without struggle. As a woman who was neither blond, blue-eyed, nor tall, she challenged the standards of the beauty hierarchy. At the age of thirty-eight, she ran into another hurdle. Her husband died suddenly, leaving her as sole supporter of their daughter.

MID-LIFE IS LIFE THAT IS HALF BEGUN—ONLY MORE. I HAVE MORE OF EVERYTHING, MORE FREEDOM, MORE COMPASSION, MORE DARING, MORE COURAGE, MORE OF THE THINGS TO BE WHO I AM.

—*Dayle Haddon*

Then, as she approached fifty, she found herself living in the middle of a throwaway, youth-struck society that discarded its older women, or at best treated them as if they were deaf and dumb. They became invisible.

WHEN I WAS YOUNGER, THERE WASN'T MUCH TO ME. IT WAS MORE ABOUT MY FACE AND MY BODY. I DIDN'T HAVE ENOUGH LIVING TO COME THROUGH, I WAS SO SHY. TODAY THERE'S SO MUCH LIVING BEHIND ME THAT BURSTS THROUGH MY SKIN. HOW YOU FEEL IS REFLECTED IN YOUR SKIN. YOU CAN'T HIDE IT.

—*Dayle Haddon*

Andre Rau/Sygma

She chose to tackle the ageism head on. Armed with statistics and a passionate voice, she once again knocked on the glittery doors of the beauty industry. She argued that it should not ignore the plight of a generation of baby boomer women. The heads of industry listened to the numbers she plied. In the meantime, she herself was determined to reach the hearts and souls of the women reaching middle age.

She formed Dayle Haddon Concepts, a company dedicated to researching and communicating issues in women's health. "I attempted to carve out an affirmation that the older you get, the better you are. Midlife is life that is half begun. I have more of everything, more freedom, more compassion, more daring, more courage, more of the things to be who I am."

She doesn't regret not being in her twenties. Being fifty is better than not being at all. And "the only thing that makes sense to me is to be truly alive."

She also wrote and published *Ageless Beauty*. The book divides the maintenance of beauty into two parts, physical, outer beauty, and spiritual, inner beauty.

"The big five-O is a marking point. It's a review of the life I've lived. "It's a celebration of the losses and the wins, of coming through the losses and acquiring the wins."

Her women friends are the ones who have helped her through to this stage, and so it was appropriate for them to be by her side to "welcome in the next fifty years."

IF YOU OBSESS ON A WRINKLE YOU'RE GOING TO LOSE.

—*Dayle Haddon*

III Joy

MADELINE URANECK

DECEMBER 30, 1947

Madeline Uraneck planned her fiftieth year with exultant expectations but lived it with a vigorous dose of reality. "I had more fun planning for the year than the year itself. [It turned out] no matter what you plan you still have to wash your clothes and go to work."

Honesty and humor overflow to all parts of her life. Because she is so prolific in ideas and so profuse in sharing, it surprised no one that she made an arm's length list of ways to celebrate fifty.

She would:

♦ write to the fifty most important people in her life
♦ do fifty new things
♦ hold a three-day celebration

- run the Stockholm marathon
- invest in people older than she
- invest in younger people, and
- " be a [size] 10 by Christmas"

She might also have listed this: "I'm finished with men; I'm doing world peace instead," but that was an end point in a several-year change of her own attitude.

She did pare the list down a little—"do fifty new things" went by the wayside and "be a 10" was never that important. What things she did do, she infused with wry, self-deprecating wisdom. At its core, each was filled with her exultant sense of living.

"Write to the fifty most important people in her life" generated a list, too, and it grew, of course, because it was Madeline's list and Madeline's lists always grow, but she defined her goal. She began the three-page, single-space letters: "It was difficult not to mix into the list of fifty those with whom I spend the most time and those I love dearly, though love greatly confounds this list. This is a list of fifty 'molders'—fifty people who were there at crucial points in my life, helped me make important decisions, pointed, usually by love and example, one way as opposed to another."

An international education consultant by profession,

she places herself in a broad community that crosses temporal and geographic boundaries. Her list included brothers and sisters, "the dead people [such as Dag Hammarksjold, Gandhi]" teachers, best friends, ex-husband, boyfriends, and "a few people you've lost the addresses to." Creating the list taught her "how many people you have to be extremely grateful for." And "you realize how many persons you are."

The letter writing was an intense exercise. "You [usually] never write a letter just saying what a person has meant and how much you love them. Here I was sitting at my computer at work and writing to my brother and I'm just sobbing. I leave tears all over these papers."

The process took the "whole bloody year. I was glad when I got to the dead people, like Gandhi, because I wouldn't have to write them."

The three-day celebration was quintessentially Madeline. She rented two cabins in the north Wisconsin woods and deliberately combined guests who had not been in the same mix before. You can get stuck in a rut with the friends you socialize with, she maintained, so it is important to create fresh relationships and mix intergenerationally.

Each family took care of a meal; everyone skied, skated,

and trekked. She gloried in being able to entertain with little responsibility. "I loved having people away from home."

The marathon was not her original idea. A friend who wanted to run the Stockholm marathon persuaded her to join. She did, but with a different intent.

"It's fun to run and compete as an older person. We only do things we're good at and it's interesting to do something you're bad at. I would always be last or next to last. There's something Zen about that."

She achieved a kind of warped pride. "There's humility [in being last]. Everyone loves you, so it's okay to come in last. Everyone would root for me. I redefined running."

To invest in those older than herself, she wrote a family

history titled "100 White Horses & 50 Comic Books or How Our Aunt Anne Met Her Guy."

To invest in the young, she went through this line of thinking: "It dawned on me that I don't have children. I can choose [my children] and invest in young people." The year she turned fifty, she told her eleven-year old nieces she would take them to France.

In truth, this wise, wisecracking, wondrous woman, who unleashes a sharp wit, could be everyone's ageless aunt. Although she used fifty as an excuse to celebrate, she created laughter and celebration for her friends. Her journal of that year often began with entries like this: "exultant Saturday, skiing, potluck with . . ."

She looks like anyone's brown-haired, slightly eccentric relative with a twinkle in her eye. She is, underneath, a poet, dancer, comedienne, and social activist who creates a magical existence in a tiny, rented lakeside cabin. Prominent in the cabin are knickknacks of Japan and Sweden—two of the countries whose languages she wants to learn, among her goal of five. Sun streams in through uncovered windows and the friends stream in through the doors that are never locked. The cabin is ever ready to let in twenty and never to bulge.

On Turning 50 ...

A good age for a woman, round, strong, definite. When one can be fully oneself, both ferocious and gentle, eccentric and ordinary. When heroines of feminism (Eleanor Roosevelt) replace those of femininity (Jackie Kennedy). Potent.

In this Year of the Tiger, I'm making time to write thank-you notes to 50 persons who helped bring me to this point of 50-ness. You are one.

It was difficult not to mix into the list of 50 those with whom I spend the most time these days, and those I love dearly, though love greatly con- founds this list. This is a list of 50 "molders"—50 people who were there at crucial points in my life, helped me make important decisions, pointed, usually by love and example, one way as opposed to another.

On my list of 50, your name shines out:

DALE R. JORDAN

Seventh and eighth grade shimmer in my memory. Today my parents say, "she had a crush on that teacher." I disagree. It was greater than a crush. It was a Midwestern, Osage County, Deweyian, Socratic mix: gadfly and student, mentor and student. It was my first heady taste of adulthood: having a grown-up, a non-parent, recognize one's abilities, challenge one, with affection and humor, to stretch tall.

You were a teacher who gave integrity to our days and integration to our learning. You were unafraid of teens, of parents, of school boards. (Were you really?) I think you were 27—old enough then but remarkably young from my vantage point today. I would have liked to have seen your journal, for surely there were more doubts and crises than you let on.

From Madeline Uraneck's letter to one of the fifty most important people in her life.

Her fiftieth was not a celebration of self. "I went to some fiftieth-birthday parties; I thought they were very indulgent. You can be celebrated when you're dead, but when you're fifty and affluent and have your health you should thank people and be working hard for the next generation."

She started inspiring the next generation when she realized she would stop running after men. Married once for about five years, "I've been a very active man chaser my whole life. I was going up to these guys out of habit. I answered personals and nothing ever came up but hilarious stories.

"How could I have spent so much time chasing men, throwing myself on men? I'll take that same energy, I think, and go for world peace or something."

The justification would follow. A young girl said to her, "I told my mother when I grow up I would like to be just like you—not married and traveling around the world."

OTTOLINE LYME*

APRIL 6, 1944

*O*ttoline Lyme was pregnant on the morning she turned fifty. Later that year, her twin boys were born. "Being a single working mother is hard and wonderful," she said. "At fifty, I'm more patient, more grateful, and I know I can get through seemingly impossible times because I already have, once or twice."

*Ottoline Lyme is the pseudonym of a writer.

Marching Band Madness

HOWARD GOURWITZ

JULY 20, 1948

*D*aily at 2 P.M. in the fall of 1998, Howard Gourwitz closed his office door and began to strip off his navy pin-striped suit. He would step into sweatpants, sneakers, and University of Michigan T-shirt, then hurry past the silver-trimmed plaque that read, "LAW OFFICES, GOURWITZ AND BARR." He was headed for band rehearsal, his briefcase and computer in hand and a suit bag flapping as he ran.

The fifty-year-old had auditioned for and had been accepted into the fall season of one of the premier collegiate marching bands of the country. He couldn't wait to eat up the miles on the forty-five-minute drive to the University of Michigan campus. "Drive carefully, have a good practice," the security guard would say, as if talking to a teenager.

He felt like a teenager. "I was excited and I always rushed." But he had a perspective most teenagers didn't have. "I was thrilled virtually every day because I realized I was doing something that nobody else was doing." He was living his dream—playing for his alma mater, reliving his days in his favorite college activity, and marking several milestones at once: his own fiftieth and the one-hundredth anniversary of the band and its fight song.

Throughout the football season, he walked on air. He glowed. "I'm having the time of my life. And you know what, I know it, too. I'm the luckiest man in the world."

He conceived of the idea as a challenge—could he train and qualify for a band of four hundred select eighteen- and twenty-year olds, practice two hours a day, and memorize new music and formations each week? Could he sustain grueling Saturdays that began with a 7 A.M. practice and on-the-field performances in temperatures ranging from 20 to 90 degrees? Could he take the pressure of weekly intraband tryouts—the Challenges—for the pregame and half-time shows?

Music had been his love from elementary school. "Growing up, my heroes were Duke Ellington and athletes." Later, he was entranced by a concert by the University of

Michigan Symphonic Band. "From ninth grade on, I always wanted to be in the Michigan band. It was so exciting to go hear that band at such a high level." Always a realist, he ruled out music as a major. "I knew I wasn't good enough. I knew my limitations." Yet high school and university marching bands thrilled him, especially because they intersected at his two loves, music and sports.

Bob Kalmbach

His intellect propelled him in another direction, however. He majored in political science and graduated from the University of Michigan in three years. After law school, he formed a practice that represented professional sports players—what he couldn't do in sports, he could do by representing its athletes.

At fifty, however, he discarded vicarious pleasure. He wanted a jolting, complete immersion. He threw away reality for six heady months and gave himself to a romantic dream. He was completing a cycle. "I always said I would get that fourth [undergraduate year]. It took me a long time to get it, but here I am."

For the sixteen months before tryouts, he ran three miles a day and, for the first time, listened seriously to the trainer he had been going to for twelve years. He took saxophone lessons. He practiced. He marked yard lines in his basement, and invited the band's drum major to put him through the paces there. "I wanted a personal challenge for turning fifty, something to jump-start the next fifty. I could have run a marathon or climbed a mountain, but those were easy."

Fifty was a threshold and a new mind-set. "I think of myself as being a very young man. When I was growing up,

fifty was a middle-aged or old person." Through his training he lost fifty pounds and obviated the need for blood
pressure medication. "I felt I could never lose. I would still
have the benefit of being in shape."

On a windy and cold November night, he practices out
on the frozen asphalt with four hundred undergraduates.
Between numbers, he stretches. The cold stiffens him. He
has to put out a different effort than the kids. "It's not natural for me to march anymore; it's not natural for me to
play anymore." The kids, he said, can be overweight and
out of shape and yet they can pull what they need out of
their bodies. They can live it up Friday and appear for
Saturday warm-ups at 7 A.M. Not he; not anymore. But
with wisdom and care, he can do everything they can.

His pleasure is intensified in the same way he concen-
trates his energies on the field, because he knows he represents the dreams of many. Spectators cheer for him; and
policemen on the street, who recognize him because of the
silvery sideburns under his cap, tell him they are rooting
for him because "we're the old guys."

In the rituals and customs that surround Saturday football games, a piece of American culture, he is content—
no, thrilled—to play the part of the musician. The lawyer

marches with not quite the snap of his comrades and his knees lift an inch lower than those who are younger than his own children. Instead he steps with economy. With no motion wasted, he makes it to the right place at the right time.

If you glance at his face, there is not a youthful vim, but an equally pure expression of beatific certainty. A far-away smile lingers on his lips. It is ecstasy.

"The best part of it, I've proved you're never too old to dream. There's no reason to compromise on your dreams."

Chef for a Day

HOWARD ALT

AUGUST 28, 1944

*T*hey called him "Dr. A" in the kitchens, so Howard Alt named his restaurant for a night "Dr. A's." When it opened, Howard Alt was nourishing not only his friends but himself. Cooking, for the psychiatrist, meant a spectrum of smells, tastes, and textures that fully opened his sensory awareness and comforted him. To serve friends food made by his hands continued what he offered in his profession—a moment of love for his patients.

"For my fiftieth I set the challenge of opening up a restaurant for a night. I would invite forty friends, have a menu, and use my family as staff." In the summer of 1994, he rented a professional kitchen at a seminary and served a four-course meal.

The menu constituted fine dining at its best: a pre-

CHEF FOR A DAY

appetizer of *Amuse Guele* followed by a first course of Fall Wild Mushroom Ragoût or Smoked Vegetable Terrine, a fish course of Seared Scallops with Caramelized Shallots, Cilantro, and Watercress, and a meat course of Duck Breast with Red Wine Reduction, Garlic Potatoes, Roasted Corn, and Sautéed Courgettes or Balsamic Marinated Filet of Beef on Sautéed Greens with Caramelized Leeks, Garlic, and Roasted Pumpkin Puree, finishing with a Mesclun Salad.

For the dessert and coffee course, guests were invited across the street to his home.

His announcement-invitation was a mock-up of a glossy magazine cover. It featured a picture of him at his stove. "Howard Alt, chef at the up and coming Dr. A's, perfecting his stock," read the caption.

Inside was the actual invitation: "Dr. A's, acclaimed one of the top twenty new restaurants in town. Make your reservations now for the special dinner honoring the chef's fiftieth birthday."

THERE IS THE SENSE AT FIFTY TO HAVE WISDOM, RESOURCES, AND DISCIPLINE TO FINISH THOSE DREAMS AND NOT HAVE DREAMS ANYMORE. THEY'RE NOT GNAWING. YOU MAKE THEM INTO A REALNESS. IT'S NOT CLOSURE, IT'S AN OPENING. YOU'RE CONNECTING WITH PARTS OF SOMETHING REALLY TRUE INSIDE.

—*Howard Alt*

43

Best New Restaurants

Dr. A's

2203 Orrington, Evanston

Howard Alt, Chef at this new restaurant, brings together a wide range of influences (Asian, Italian, Mexican) into a coherent selection of dishes. This, combined with the warmth and attention to service, provide for a mix of elegance, sophistication and home feeling.

Dr. A's

Acclaimed one of the top 20 new restaurants in town.

Make your reservations now for the special dinner honoring the Chef's 50th Birthday.

Saturday Sept. 10
6:30 p.m.

331

Dr. A's

Saturday, September 10th, 1994
50th Birthday Celebration

~

Amuse-Huele

—

Fall Wild Mushroom Ragoût
or
Smoked Vegetable Terrine

—

Seared Scallops with carmelized
Shallots, Cilantro and Watercress

—

Duck Breast with Red Wine Reduction,
Garlic Potatoes, Roasted Corn and
Sautéed Courgettes
or
Balsamic Marinated Filet of Beef on
Sautéed greens, with carmelized leeks,
garlic and roasted pumpkin puree

~

Mesclun salad with Pecans, Maytag Blue
in Vinegarette

~

Assorted Desserts and Coffee to follow at The
home of Jane and Howard

His inspiration came out of a desire not to be the center of attention. "I don't like having everyone come and having a surprise and being the center of attention. I wanted to do something myself," he said.

The restaurant idea grew out of a natural chain of events. For about five years before his fiftieth he had apprenticed himself to two nationally renowned chefs in Chicago. "Five years ago, I wanted to kick it up a notch. What if I take a day off? I had always taken a day off for gardening. Why don't I see if I can make connections and volunteer at some restaurants?" Thus began a habit of working in restaurants on Friday nights. Young kitchen hands liked him, and coined the affectionate "Dr. A" for this older, volunteer cook who worked shoulder to shoulder with them.

> I LIKE LIVING. I THINK IT'S A GAS, EVEN WITH ITS ANXIETY AND DEPRESSION.
>
> —Howard Alt

Cooking itself boiled over from a boyhood love. "In seventh grade, I formed a gourmet club; I wanted to move beyond Chef Boyardee pizzas." Even at middle age, he takes cookbooks to bed as reading material.

He relates cooking to psychiatry this way: "I love the experience; I enjoy the essence of people coming and having a good time—like Rick's Club in the movie *Casablanca*. There's some chefs who love that emergency feeling. For me cooking is peaceful, soothing. You put on some music,

go to the basement to get ancho [peppers], and open up a box and these smells rise up." Unlike the chefs who revel in a jolt of adrenaline—"I don't become vivid"—the shy, scholarlike psychiatrist finds that

IN YOUR TWENTIES AND THIRTIES YOU'RE COMPETING, FOR SECURITY, FOR MONEY, EGO. THERE'S SOMETHING THAT'S RELIEVING ABOUT YOUR FIFTIES. THERE'S THE SENSE THAT I'VE GOTTEN THROUGH THE MAJORITY OF MY LIFE AND IT'LL BE OKAY.

—Howard Alt

through food "I can express myself and bring myself together. There's a good peaceful, contented, full feeling."

In psychiatry, "the essence is connecting with the other person. You look for some energy to develop. Both [cooking and psychiatry] are caretaking . . . I like to go to a place where there's a sense of being held in the experience of being treated. People feel excited, people feel warm. It comes together in a small restaurant."

He was feeling a general contentment. A few years before he turned fifty, he was thought to have a heart prob-

lem. ("I was probably awful to live with.") The health anxieties were resolved and relief set in, yet because of the scare, he had been propelled to get in better shape. As his fiftieth approached, "I was back in life. It was kind of an opening up of things."

The marker itself meant less to him than the challenge. "The fiftieth birthday gave me an excuse to do an endeavor. Those markers are times when you are given permission to express some authenticness of who you are and to make a statement on that. It is an opportunity for an authentic explosion."

IV Gratitude

LINDA ELLERBEE

AUGUST 15, 1944

I n my prayers I was afraid to ask 'please let me live a long life,' so instead I asked, 'please let me live to see fifty,'" said Linda Ellerbee, journalist and head of Lucky Duck Productions. She had been diagnosed with breast cancer at age forty-seven and she coped by limiting her hopes. An award-winning television producer and author, she has won numerous Emmy awards for writing and is especially known for producing *Nick News*, a children's news program.

She would lose both breasts to surgery. "All of a sudden the idea of turning fifty was the most appealing thing in the world. On the day I turned fifty, I felt more victorious than I did when I turned twenty-one."

Her friends celebrated her birthday with fantastic

fun—"wild-ass things" as she described it. Thirty of them donned Linda Ellerbee masks and lay in wait to surprise her. T-shirts were made that listed famous people born on her birthday as well as events that occurred on that day. "It was like having your own scrapbook on your T-shirt."

The signal event of her fiftieth, however, was not loud. She took off on a solo backpacking trip, a ritual she has continued for five years, with the duration of each trip increasing each year. She started with a one-day hike, but now has extended it to almost a week. It renews her like nothing else. "I find that being able to climb the mountain and being able to take care of myself and wake up on my birthday on something I've climbed gives me a shot of adrenaline that's better than anybody telling me 'you're not getting older, you're getting better,'" said the woman with a chocolatey-rich broadcast voice.

"I find physical and spiritual comfort in the woods."

That voice is vigorous beyond its professional patina. It carries a vibrant, ecstatic undertone where a laugh always lurks. "Here I am, a middle-aged, pear-shaped woman slowly going up the hill." Gratitude exudes from her words. "I ask myself what other hills in my life, that I don't think I can climb, can I get to? This translated into helping me overcome cancer."

The solo retreat challenges her at the same time that it feeds her soul. "It's me and my thoughts and the ability to carry everything I need on my back—my shelter and my food. I can stop anywhere I choose and take care of myself—and enjoy both the physical beauty and

AS FAR AS FIFTY GOES, I'VE BEEN TO THAT HORIZON. I'VE BEEN UP THAT HILL, AND THE VIEW IS STILL GOOD . . . THE HORIZON IS NOT LIMITLESS, BUT IT'S STILL A LONG, LONG WAY AWAY.

—*Linda Ellerbee*

Rolfe Tessem

spiritual calm that comes with that and the feeling of confidence of being able to take care of myself in the woods." At the core, it is not achievement but communion that she cherishes. "The older I get, the more I need that physical beauty around me. There's something in my soul that needs larger doses of that every year."

She has scaled peaks and hiked trails she never thought she could, a crucial metaphor that also tells her there are more peaks and trails to explore. "You become aware that there are not an unlimited number of summers, not even of Saturday nights. How much are you going to be putting off?"

She feels a gratitude that spills into an overwhelming zest for life. "I take off from work every minute that I can take off from work—of course, it helps to have your own company . . ."

The cancer scare has been a wake-up call. "As far as fifty goes, I've been to that horizon. I've been up that hill, and the view is still good. The horizon is not limitless, but it's still a long, long way away."

STEVEN PRATT

NOVEMBER 3, 1944

O n his fiftieth, Steve Pratt and his wife laid down the plans for how they would retire to Florida, yet soon after, she died suddenly. Deeply grieved, he still accepted the financial freedom that befell him as a result of her death. He sold their house, walked out of his job, and headed for the Florida Keys. "I had more things that I wanted to do with my life than spend it at a desk until I was unable to do anything else."

It was her gift to him.

In time, he sent an e-mail to their friends informing them that the yacht he had bought had been painted with an official name, his wife's.

"She was always Joy . . ."

I HAD MORE THINGS THAT I WANTED TO DO WITH MY LIFE THAN SPEND IT AT A DESK UNTIL I WAS UNABLE TO DO ANYTHING ELSE. THAT'S WHEN I VERY SERIOUSLY STARTED TO PLAN THE ESCAPE.

—*Steven Pratt*

Planting Willows

VIRGINIA REYNOLDS

For days before her birthday, Virginia Reynolds, whose chosen profession is housecleaning, cleaned her own home with barely suppressed excitement. "It was having everybody under one roof. I had made a half century. So many times it could have gone under—through all those ups and downs we had made it as a family. I was just tickled."

She called her children and friends to remind them, although three months before she had already asked them to be present to "commemorate my fiftieth." On the given day, her four children, their spouses, three grandchildren, and a handful of friends gathered for a summer's ranch feast in Wells, Nevada.

The prologue occurred three days earlier, when her son

planted willow trees on her farm, two acres that she had carved out of semiarid land and cultivated into a verdant paradise. She had asked her children for the willows. "Willow was significant to me for being willing to bend. By the time you're fifty you have to learn how to bend because life will either bend or break you." Willow roots grow toward water, and she now was keeper of a piece of land with large ponds where willows could flourish.

They feasted. The remains of barbecued beef and potato salad littered the picnic table, and the brown, sweet stain of molasses-baked beans smudged the paper plates. After the cake, son Daniel, twenty-one, teasingly shouted "speech." His mother rose to her full five feet two inches, her bare feet planted in grass. The desert evening sucked up the sound of fifteen pairs of clapping hands. Her children and grandchildren filled her gaze. For all the joy she knew and for the control she had exercised in planning the event, she was unprepared for the personal outpouring that rode over the cacophony of a farm silence.

"I stood up and realized the dream that I had had since I was a little girl had manifested. I was looking out at four beautiful children and grandchildren and thanking them for coming through me. There they were. They were exquisite."

She thanked them, speaking from the Native American philosophy that she, of European descent, had been learning. "My children know my belief system. They chose me to be their mother. I thanked them for coming and going through some really hard times and choosing to walk this life with me as their mother. What a privilege it was to have them come through me.

"I realized that I had had the dream of living on a farm and having a family. From nothing to everything. I thanked friends for walking a few paths with me. I realized how grateful I was to have this life. I was blessed." She wept, and for a moment, the farm and her family wept with her.

She had been "one of those women with obscene histories," her life "a bad B-movie." She ran away from home at sixteen, married, and gave birth to a clubfooted baby. Shortly after, her husband was jailed. She replaced him with an abusive alcoholic and eventually left him. For the following five years, she supported her children by working in casinos. She then married a college-educated man and gave birth to two more children. With this marriage she had the long-dreamed-of brick house and white picket fence, but circumstances forced her to leave her children home and work three jobs. At the same time, her husband was diagnosed

EVERY WRINKLE I'VE GOT, I
ADORE. I EARNED THEM.

—*Virginia Reynolds*

with epilepsy and she began to care for him.

Desperate to be June Cleaver since she was a girl, she spun ever-widening rings of despair around herself. By 1988, she was hospitalized with a mental breakdown as her marriage ended. Later, she married again and began to renovate a historic dairy farm on the outskirts of Wells, a town of 1,100. The site contains a natural hot spring where she has built a Native American sweat lodge and where she leads healing sessions.

Daily she celebrates the rituals and rhythms of an older woman. She rises at 4:30 A.M., writes, then feeds the menagerie: chickens, ducks, peacock, two catfish, four barn cats, and dogs. She takes care of the grounds and gardens, and by afternoon she goes out to clean others' houses.

"When I was a young woman I would have given anything to come home one day a week to a clean house. It's not a survival mechanism to make money, but a gift to younger women." The job also represents her own spiritual work: "When you're cleaning somebody else's toilet your ego cannot get out of line."

She cherishes her role as an elder. "Native philosophy is that a woman does not become fully mature until she reaches fifty-two. At fifty-two you can look at younger women and understand their wringing of the hands. You stop hitting yourself for the things you did."

Entering old age is not the terror of wrinkles but the wisdom to be bemused and to listen—to wait for the daughters to come to her with questions, to give her granddaughters another perspective. "Every wrinkle I've got, I adore. I earned them."

ROBBY GREENBERG

JUNE 28, 1948

*R*obby Greenberg held two gatherings on the weekend she turned fifty, one private and one public.

The second, larger one was easy: a music party on the beach and a personal benefit for her clients, the developmentally disabled. It flowed naturally out of her lifestyle and work. As founder of the local folk music club and director of the annual folk festival in the Fort Lauderdale area, she and her husband, Steve, often threw musical parties at home. "Every year, we invite people to 'our party,' which was at our house with friends bringing guitars and food to share."

For her fiftieth though, "I wanted to give back."

This time, she reversed the usual potluck. She asked

that guests bring no food and no presents for her; instead, she asked them to give to her clients. This, too, was routine in her professional life. "I try to get services donated—like dental work and clothing—but I realized that fifty people networking could probably do much more than I could in a short amount of time to locate fun things for my clients."

Her invitation read, "Bring your musical instruments and bathing suits." And "Gifts are not on the agenda, but if you must, please bring something appropriate for one of my clients."

I APPRECIATE MY WOMEN FRIENDS AT FIFTY. THEY SHOW MORE INTROSPECTION. I APPRECIATE THE CARE WOMEN SHOW THE WORLD.

—*Robby Greenberg*

The gifts flowed in. Later, she sent out thank-you notes. "On behalf of my clients, thank you all!" She listed the gifts: "Movie passes from Al, seats at a Marlins' game with [hosts] the Londons, $$ for meals from Debbie and Jim, holiday concert tickets, Discovery Center and IMAX tickets from Laura Sue . . ."

The celebration seemed an easy and natural expression of a woman who was a soul of the '60s, albeit a timid one. She would turn out for candlelight peace vigils at college. She wanted passionately to join Martin Luther King's march on Selma but didn't, and "wouldn't have gotten permisssion anyway." She knew she wanted to work with the disabled but was derailed by a baby and a divorce. Then followed almost ten years of working in her family's restaurant.

It wasn't until she turned forty that "I found my way back to what I wanted to be." A perfect job in social services, a new marriage, and a chance to mingle with folk singers began a decade of singing from her soul that she doesn't expect to end. Her favorite folk songs, she said, are "story songs, uplifting songs. They encourage you to go out in the world and do wonderful things."

As much as her beach party's theme was giving back, she took life force from a small gathering held on the

50 ON THE BEACH

Please join Steve and me for my 50th birthday on June 27 at 6 PM at Sea Ranch Club Condominiums, 5100 N Ocean Blvd, Ft Laud in the Beachhouse

Bring your musical instruments and bathing suits.

Gifts are not on the agenda, but if you must, please bring something appropriate for one of my clients. As most of you know, I work with adults with mental retardation. Some things they might like are cos... ps or sports paraphe... taxi, IMA... Discove... R...

On behalf of my clients, thank you all!

- movie passes from Al
- seats at a Marlin's game with the Londons
- engineer cap from Amy Carol & Brooke
- clothes & "geeky shoes" from Liz & Zig
- $$ for meals from Mom & Dad
- $$ for meals from Debbie & Jim
- Holiday Concert tickets, Discovery Center & IMAX tickets from Laura Sue
- charity basketball game tix from Monica & Sara
- lots of costume jewelry from my mother-in-law, Eleanor M
- lots of little bottles of body lotions, nail polish, shower gel, etc from Merle
- clothes from Stu & Pam

- beauty cream and shower gel from Kelli & Nick
- 30 tickets for the water bus from Grace, Joe, Billy, Dave & Mary Jo

Thanks also to Dave H for the cheese plate, Eden & Dan for the homus & veggie plate, Susan for the potato salad, Liz for the lemonade, Steve for the greek salad, Dad for the homemade bread, and Peggy for my birthday cake!

Thanks to all of you who pitched in to help! Thanks to my parents for sharing their beach house & ocean!

And thanks to all of my wonderful friends for being my wonderful friends!

Love,

Robby

Friday before. While the beach party drew out the lines of her '60s conscience, she also wanted something retro: a slumber party. Six women friends were invited and the gathering took place in the home of the one who was single. The host asked each woman beforehand to name her comfort food and, as well, to bring a nonfood comfort. The reason: "Many of us don't take time to take care to do nurturing things for ourselves."

And so, for dinner, they were served six formal courses: a Nestlé's Milk Chocolate Bar (in the *red* wrapper), chocolate ice cream, mint chocolate chip ice cream, a Cuban pound cake with condensed milk and whipped cream, popcorn, and Fritos with spinach dip. The host, in a desperate, last-minute attempt to inject something healthy, pulled out a Kalamata olive spread.

In sharing nonfood comforts, one friend, a schoolteacher, read a story of a New England woman who planted flowers all over her town. The masseuse gave massages. One brought her favorite CD, and as the women finished eating, they began to move to the music. "We danced wildly."

Robby brought the folk song she had written to her daughter when she was fifteen. It was, she said, a love song from a mother to a daughter.

Neighbors in for cake and coffee, meeting at my place
Baby at my breast, reaches up to touch my face

Next summer in my garden, Midwest sun upon my back
She toddles over to me, lifts her arms to hug my neck
She shows me in her own sweet way, just how much she
   loves me
She shows me in her own sweet way, just how much she
   cares . . .

Years later in the winter, she's called me to her side
There's a newborn baby in her arms, tears are in her eyes
He shows her in his own sweet way, just how much she
   cares.

As she said, folk songs have the power to "encourage you to go out in the world and do wonderful things."

V Compassion

RON KLEIN

Not one of them knew his birthdate, but when fifty of Ron Klein's friends each received fifty dollars from him, they were not surprised. The enclosed handwritten message characterized him perfectly: "Help me celebrate my fiftieth birthday. Do something nice for yourself, for me," it read.

Of course they were astonished by the gift itself, the snapping, crisp bill that tumbled out of the envelope from Japan. Yet they knew Ron as a person who perennially pushed to think and act outside of the norm. They knew him as a creative person who asked of his friends to live their lives the same way.

The gift and the secret birthday both show how the man regards the art and practice of living outside convention so that celebration, growth, and journey continually unfold.

"I haven't celebrated my birthday publicly for twenty years. I think just celebrating your birthday once a year is sort of unfortunate. I found that most people are disappointed on their birthdays. They expect certain things from certain people."

The secret birthdate "allows me to celebrate the way I want, with whom I want, or not, whenever I want. I really programmed myself not to bother myself on a particular day." It releases him from inappropriate parties, conversations, and presents. "I just get out of that loop."

He lives outside the loop. In early 1997, he looked at a list of yearly goals by category: work, family, relationship, personal travel, and wealth. This was a ritual for the man who now teaches English at a women's college in Japan. "When I got to wealth, I thought, why don't I share the wealth? I am single and I am paid a good salary so I have more money than I need and feel an obligation to give some of it away."

He had struggled financially for most of his life. "We all have our poor stories. The bag of bread crust ends, hitchhiking, calling different friends for dinner." His lean days continued well past graduate student days. With a doctorate in Creativity from the School of Education, University of Massachusetts, he had thought, "Every school of ed would want someone teaching creativity." No one did.

He lit on a series of part-time jobs in arts administration, led workshops in creative thinking, and produced several global New Age events of the '70s. By 1987, he found himself stably situated as director of communications at a junior college. He was forty. That year, as he examined his list of goals, he had written under Work, "I quit." And under Personal, "travel." The two together made sense. He left his job with his boss's words in his ears: "What are you going to be when you grow up?"

He didn't know, but at forty, growth was exactly what he sought. "You have to take a break, create a discontinuity. There are stages where you either grow or die. You reach a point where you replicate, mutualize [spin off], and then you spin out, unless you have a catastrophe that forces you to change."

"I didn't have it so I had to create discontinuity. And then I would come back and start the back forty."

The back forty began with the self-promised journey, twelve months that became eighteen. It included hiking

Mount Everest and walking the Great Wall of China. Eventually, "the outer journey turned into the inner journey." At a monastery stop in Tibet, he recalled another monastery he had discovered in Japan. He returned to it. "I checked into the Zen temple, and that was almost ten years ago."

At age fifty, he is where he wants to be, but never wants to finish growing. He has found a master, a practice, and a milieu that suit him. "I had been on the spiritual path for many, many years, and hung out in New Age circles since before it was New Age, but I had never had my own practice."

His idea of the back forty has stretched to the back fifty, "a midpoint," and not a threshold to old age. He fully expects to live to a hundred. Thus, he re-created another midpoint journey. "The challenge of my fiftieth year was my summer trip to Mount Kailash, a sacred holy mountain in southwestern Tibet. It's a brutal journey—to the end of the earth kind of thing—a four-thousand-kilometer journey over land on dirt roads."

In the meantime, small celebrations of his fiftieth were taking place. The responses from the recipients of his fiftieth-year celebration gifts delighted him with their ingenuity.

They were ordinary acts become celebrations for the meaning they lent to the daily lives of his friends. His creativity and generosity begat theirs. Leandra, fourteen, bought a prom dress; her mother, Cindy, contributed half of her own gift from Ron toward Leandra's prom transportation, the other toward a friend's sweat lodge; Sally, in England, bought her marriage license; Lynne planted flowers in the front of her house; Karen got a tattoo; Rob took his family disco bowling, and Steve bought a swing set that led to a remodeling of his backyard to make it safer for Emily, his autistic eight-year-old.

These became the gifts for someone who considers himself a catalyst for creativity, but whose own birthdate remains, as he insists, inconsequential. What matters is what he causes to happen. "What really tickled me was how serious they were about doing something nice for themselves."

Scholarship by Wager

BURT SAXON

JUNE 22, 1947

*O*ne thing was certain. My fiftieth birthday party was not going to be what anthropologists call a status blood bath," Burt Saxon decided.

He had seen many big bashes. For him, though, "How could it be? An inner-city schoolteacher who has just finished sending two children through Brown and Harvard Law School is not in a position to impress anyone," he said.

"Nor did I want to."

The man who had dedicated himself to inner-city schools since college, winner of a teacher-of-the-year award in his school system as well as a state award for a voluntary desegregation program he developed, would create his own anniversary. It would suit his lifelong intention and a few other passions, chief among them athletics.

74

Tennis, baseball, basketball, football—he played them all in college. In 1996, he had begun collecting autographs of athletes by mail. He was struck by the fact that some athletes asked for a donation to their charities in return for an autograph. In particular, he noticed that Monte Irvin, a player in the Negro Leagues and later for the New York Giants, asked for contributions to his alma mater.

"It struck me that here's a guy who could have taken an attitude, 'I never earned as much money as I could have.' He could have spent the rest of his life as a Hall of Fame player, signing autographs. Instead, he raises money for Lincoln University [in Pennsylvania]."

This solved his birthday query. "My wife and I would invite friends and endow a scholarship fund at my high school for students who had finished one year of college but found money hard to come by after that."

The Ming-blue mailers that the Saxons sent out began "Celebrate the end of the school year with a Chinese buffet, a scholarship drive, and a birthday party."

He set a goal of ten thousand dollars, and immediately his mother, brother, and son contributed enough to reach more than half that amount. The sixty colleagues and family who attended the meal donated enough to bring the sum

CELEBRATE THE END OF THE SCHOOL YEAR

- with a Chinese buffet
  - a scholarship drive
    - a birthday party

In honor of Burt Saxon's 50th Birthday, we are starting THE HILLHOUSE FAMILY SECOND YEAR SCHOLARSHIP. This fund will go to a Hillhouse High School graduate who wants to continue college after successfully completing his or her freshman year.

We hope that you will come and celebrate with us on Sunday, the 22nd of June at the Fortune Pavilion next to Caldor's in the Caldor Shopping Center located on Route 34 in Derby, from 1:30 to 4:30 pm.

Instead of presents for Burt's birthday, we ask that you send your tax-deductible check for $20 (or more) per person to get this fund underway. Our goal is to raise $10,000 to endow this scholarship.

Join us on the 22nd of June.
The party and food are on Myra.
Education is on all of us!

R.S.V.P. by June 18th to: or   Althea Norcott
Myra Saxon   Hillhouse High School
411 Richard Lane
Orange, CT 06477
(203) 795-9628

Make checks out to: HILLHOUSE FAMILY SECOND YEAR SCHOLARSHIP

only twenty-one hundred dollars short of the goal.

It was a friend who gave Burt a gift that made up the sum, although it was Burt who paid it. "It was an offer I could not refuse," for it was an athletic test. "He challenged me to a doubles tennis match in which he guaranteed that my partner would be a little better than his partner. The loser would write the last twenty-one-hundred-dollar check."

On Labor Day weekend, at age fifty, he played against his forty-year-old friend. His friend's team won in the third set, 6 to 4. It was, though, by all accounts, a victory. I played the best tennis I ever played." Furthermore, "I had figured all along I'd write the check for the last piece."

His Hillhouse High School Scholarship for second-year college students aims for humble but laudable goals. The interest on ten thousand dollars brings little money,

"maybe a hundred dollars to everybody who asks." However, he knew that although inner-city high school graduates might receive large first-year scholarships, they are not always supported similarly for the second year. With social and familial pressures, the drop-out rate is high. His scholarship, though small, "may have the effect of bringing kids back, and we can be supportive and encouraging [to them]."

He had succeeded in avoiding the status game. He didn't become an inner-city teacher for status.

"Teaching is like some of the other social service professions. You're known to a small amount of people. It's not a high-profile profession." He rather measures his profile by the times he is stopped on the street by people who tell him they remember him. "Rather than have your name in the paper, what you can hope for is you have touched a small number of people and sometimes in ways you don't realize, sometimes profound."

78

SUSAN RASKIN

JUNE 7, 1949

$\int$usan Raskin found herself shadowed by death as she approached fifty. The death of her stepmother of forty years, the deaths of her father- and brother-in-law, and the news that her mother-in-law suffered from a brain tumor and a recurrence of lung cancer struck blows she found hard to absorb.

There was more. Her husband wanted a divorce; and the business she had started—a Web site called Prime Choices—was not a financial success.

She would rise above this surround of death, this excess of drama, as fifty approached. First, it took an epiphany: she awoke one morning determined to settle the divorce and take control of bringing it to a close. Suddenly, she found that in the debris of her twenty-eight-year marriage, she could be "making all these decisions about who I want to be around and what I want to do."

She was able to think about celebration again, not just filtered through the death cloud, but fully in the face of death. She remembered how mortality and life are bedfellows. "I look forward to turning fifty. My mother died of leukemia when I was six. Many women lie about their age. I'm so proud on my birthday to say I'm X number years old. I like to say the number. Every year I've lived X number of years more than my mother. I'm very lucky."

While she could have bemoaned the fact that she no longer had a husband to treat her to a lavish birthday as she had done for him, she started to create her own.

She considered throwing a huge party for her women friends. Many had already held spectacular fiftieth bashes. She could do any number of "very expensive and exciting" things.

However, "all the money in the world from the divorce or an evening at a five-star restaurant doesn't mean shit when four of the people you love most in the world die. I wanted to see if I could get away from being so absorbed. I'm not a great philanthropist, but I was tired of thinking about me."

She refocused on "giving time or money to people." The idea blossomed. "I'm going to hope for a gorgeous day and see if my children can come here. We can spend the day biking, going to museums. Being with the two people in my life who are most important to me is what I want."

She proposed the get-together to her two daughters, ages twenty-two and twenty-four. Once together she would describe her idea. "I'm going to set up a fund and ask them if they want to do the same." They would call it

something like "The Raskin Girls Foundation." The funds would support research on children's health.

It felt right. She had raised her children to serve social causes. In nearly fifty years of living, she realized, she prized her own such efforts. "When I think of all the things that mean the most wonderful things in my life, it was starting a clinic for indigent women in Appalachia." She also remembered the years she worked for an AIDS clinic, which her then-teenage daughter had asked her to do.

"I had the luxury of doing other things and of helping others. I want to get back to that."

MY MOTHER DIED OF LEUKEMIA WHEN I WAS SIX . . . I'M SO PROUD ON MY BIRTHDAY TO SAY I'M X NUMBER YEARS OLD. I LIKE TO SAY THE NUMBER. EVERY YEAR I'VE LIVED X NUMBER YEARS MORE THAN MY MOTHER. I'M VERY LUCKY.

—*Susan Raskin*

VI Transformation

Skydiving into Cronehood

MELODY LENKNER

MARCH 27, 1943

As soon as she saw the banner at her local airport for tandem skydiving, Mel Lenkner hurtled in, signed up, and within a half hour, was somersaulting backward off an airplane. It was just what she had always dreamed of doing.

This redhead with the toothsome, girlish grin, who voices her thoughts in a mature, mellifluous contralto, marked fifty in her inimitable, expansive style. She rejoiced in both the youthful and the ancient to mark fifty. The dive was followed by a croning ceremony later in the year.

That first and only skydive was a divine experience. "In that time you really feel like a bird. You feel you're really being part of the world. It was one of those things that was timeless."

84

For years, "I'd been scheming to jump out of an airplane without becoming a skydiver." Miraculously, her local airport delivered the opportunity for a one-time jump in tandem with an instructor. "I'd never heard of it before and the airport was a mile away. I signed away my life [to go on the plane]. My husband was wringing his hands and he didn't even see the forms I signed."

When the dive was over, she was finished, sated, complete; it was a perfect one-time experience, not the acquisition of a skill. "It's just exactly what you'd want—none of the responsibility [of learning] and all the thrill."

In fact, hers was not a bravura, youthful act in the face of aging. She drew a very different lesson from the dive: the fact that the right opportunity came to her at the right time. "It was the beginning of understanding that if you're quiet and know what you want and don't try to force it into experience, it comes your way."

The second part of her birthday honored just such qualities of quiet clarity and patience. She held a croning ceremony, based on ancient Native American rituals, for herself and fifteen women friends. The crone is the older woman who holds within her "all the wisdom and compassion of age. And in our particular society, it's not very well honored. As women age in our culture they become nothing and invisible. Crones in other cultures are honored and esteemed. They've been through life."

She would hold the ceremony "for my women friends, myself, and my daughter." She wanted to validate the passage, as it is expressed in Native American cultures, from maiden to mother to crone. Now the skydiving woman of the '90s would connect to a timelessness of a different culture.

She invited two sets of friends who, by her own definition, were "a polyester set and a New Age set." Then she waited. Eventually, "the ones who showed were ones who belonged." On the given day, some brought gifts that matched their values. She accepted graciously a bottle of Pepto-Bismol from the polyesters, flowers and a clay necklace strung with various symbols of her lifetime from the New Agers.

Part of the initiation into cronehood is to create and prepare one's own ceremony. The process is itself a sign of maturation. "You are moving from the external to internal and recognizing what's going on in you."

To prepare for the evening, she and four close friends dug a pit in her yard and filled it with wood, which they then set ablaze. Into this earth-oven they placed a turkey and ears of corn. "The ceremonial burying of food is a symbol of connectedness to the earth." They ate first, taking food from the pit. "Cronehood is about understanding the connection of all of us together as well as to the earth. It's a real deep understanding that man did not weave the web of life, he is merely a strand in it."

Following the feast, she addressed the circle about cronehood. Then a friend placed on her red locks the crown Mel had fashioned. To "crone" a woman is to "crown" her, the first word growing out of the other.

She had given careful thought to the making of the crown. First she wove together

MY MOTHER CRIED WHEN SHE TURNED FORTY, BUT I WANT TO LIVE UNTIL I DIE. FOR ME THIS [CRONING CEREMONY] WAS THE COMMITMENT TO DO THAT. I WANTED NOT TO FALL IN THAT OLD TRAP OF TRYING TO STAY YOUNG AND BE A ROLE MODEL FOR MY DAUGHTER. I DON'T WANT HER NOT TO LOOK FORWARD TO AGING.

—Mel Lenkner

87

sage and purple cloth for the body of the crown. Onto it she attached symbols playful and profound. There were sequins, a yin-yang circle, feathers of the redtail hawk (her animal symbol according to Native American beliefs), and finally the figurine of an "outrageous girl leaping in the air, clothes falling up, red hair blowing." The last signified for her "taking risks even if it means leaving behind what you used to be," and "what I wanted to move into for my next fifty years."

With the crown on her head she asked the women to stand. Her husband lit a torch and touched the sparklers

I WOULDN'T GO BACK TO ANY OTHER AGE. YOU REALLY REALIZE YOU ARE BECOMING WHO YOU ARE. IT'S REALLY YOURS AND NO ONE ELSE'S. IT'S SO MUCH FUN.

—Mel Lenkner

88

each woman was holding. When all were lit, "we went wildly dancing and we became children again."

What followed was in some ways as sublime as the ceremony itself: "Then we went inside and had cake and ice cream."

She held the croning ceremony to validate herself in her third age; to celebrate at once her liveliness, her silliness, her divinity, and her wisdom. However, fifty does not automatically confer wisdom and intuition. "You could turn seventy-five and never reach cronehood and you could be a crone from the day you're born."

She overcame not biology, but culture to understand her own transition. "My mother cried when she turned forty, but I want to live until I die. For me this was the commitment to do that. I wanted not to fall in that old trap of trying to stay young. To be a role model for my daughter. I don't want her not to look forward to aging."

Of course, "there are days I feel like that and there are other days when I feel like I'm just getting more wrinkles." Yet without question, "this is the happiest time of my life. I wouldn't go back to any other age. You really realize you are becoming who you are. You realize your life is yours and no one else's."

Solitude in Costa Rica

LAURENCE WALSH

DECEMBER 6, 1948

aurence "Laurie" Walsh looked forward to a wild and woolly fiftieth party but when the time arrived, he found himself completely alone and grateful for the peace. "What I had dreamed of at fifty years and what I thought it would've been like was very different. [Instead,] it was very quiet, very serene, very reflective."

He had traveled to Costa Rica to help his brother, who was getting divorced, to sell his home. "I went for the adventure and when I got there I decided I didn't need the adventure. I needed to reflect.

"It was actually perfect because it was done with no alcohol, no anything. I was sitting on this beautiful hill where my brother's home is, just gazing down on the Pacific."

In looking at the dissembling of his brother's life, he was able to look on the transition in his own life.

Early in the day, he took himself to a church in San Jose. "I went to the cathedral to light candles for anyone who means anything to me." Then he drove through the countryside to what seemed to be the end of the earth. "I had put myself in one of the quietest spots on the planet."

The quiet allowed the music within to sound. "What I got out of it was a deep appreciation for the love of my family, on closeness, on rebonding with my brother."

A true journeyman, he had always sought adventure. He quit college after two years, and worked various jobs long enough to save some money. Then his curiosity would surface and he would be off again. "I worked training parrots in Hawaii, I worked in theater in upstate New York. As long as I had enough money, I had enough curiosity to travel."

His sojourns took him to Nepal, Thailand, Hong Kong, Japan, Morocco, Finland, Turkey, and the Spanish Sahara. "Mostly I stayed as long as I could."

Turkey in 1974 was a high point. "I went around the whole country and lived with the villagers and explored the mountains. I don't speak a word of Turkish—I can barely speak English." Back in the United States, he entered the real estate trade and stuck with it. Little trav-els continued, but "no real adventures."

He had expected Costa Rica to return the savor and color of his swashbuckling years. "I expected something wild and crazy. I thought we'd go out with the guys, do something that was a lot of fun." Except, it was "just me and him and that's how it was thirty years ago when we were on the north shore of Oahu. The old stuff that meant a lot is fun, but the older I get, it is not as exciting and I can't do it as well now."

Instead, he reflected on the lives of his parents and grieved over their recent deaths. For the past several years he had been their caretaker. Unmarried, he had shared a home with them and had taken care of them during their illnesses. "I got used to taking care of my parents. That was completely taken away from me and there's an absolute void. There were no kids. When I was caretaking, all the [extended] family would center around us."

The moment of grief spurred questions and reevaluation. "Everything is quite comfortable, I'm married to a woman who loves me; I have a career that I don't enjoy anymore. It's a lonely stage. I don't know how to put it together.

"I need to go in a different direction for the rest of my

life—to help other people. Without that in my life, it lacks the meaning that I want it to have."

Yet the seeds may be in place. As a Realtor, he has his hand in many building projects. "One thing I notice when I run these condo projects, I find a lot in my generation that are about to go through what I went through [having the responsibility of aging parents]. There's no place to stick them. That's one avenue I'm looking at."

WHAT I HAD DREAMED OF AT FIFTY YEARS AND WHAT I THOUGHT IT WOULD'VE BEEN LIKE WAS VERY DIFFERENT. IT WAS VERY QUIET, VERY SERENE, VERY REFLECTIVE.

—*Laurence Walsh,*
far right

Breast Reduction Surgery

PEG TAPPE

JUNE 15, 1947

Breast reduction surgery would mark Peg Tappe's entry into year fifty and her physical transformation would trigger gratitude, relief, and her ready humor. But it was only the beginning of a sea change from the inside out that would give her increasing hope.

The day of her fiftieth was ominous; it fell on Father's Day. Her father was dead but it was also her uncle's eightieth birthday, and her family honored him with a gathering. Her birthday was not noted at all. It might have symbolized her lot in life—to be unrecognized. Her family always paid scant attention to the milestones of this single woman, a guidance counselor.

She could have bent to the twisted irony. Yet, despite

the poverty of emotion shown by her family, she would mark the year with activities and deep laughter.

Besides the surgery, she became a certified scuba diver, she highlighted her hair, and she was honored at a sumptuous dinner. To all of this she brought her customary wacky sense of humor. Humor is how she always salvaged herself.

On the day she drove herself to the hospital, she wore a button she had made: "THAT'S a load off my chest." It brought the operating team to its knees.

Three weeks later, at her checkup, she strode in and announced to the surgeon, "Well, I learned something—a man's definition of small is different from a woman's. I think they're fine but I don't think they're small."

Pre-surgery, she had ordered small breasts. "I have this fantasy that [after breast reduction] I could run around in the backyard without a bra and just wear a T-shirt." That result was not quite reached, her doctor agreed.

She learned a second lesson about herself from the surgery. "When you're in the hospital the doctors and nurses are there to take care of you. I didn't expect that stuff. It was a little embarrassing to me." What comes naturally to so many was a learned response for her. "I realized that's what those people had chosen to do with their life and it was my place to accept that graciously and revel in the gift."

The girl-woman, who grew up poor, always looked after herself, bought her own clothes since seventh grade, and took care of her family, was learning to receive, including from herself. "I didn't know how I felt about spending money to alter the way I look." The result of the surgery was more than cosmetic. It was "a huge freeing thing. I used to have lower back and neck pain. I wished I'd done it twenty years before."

However, she felt gratitude and not regret for the belated chance. She had been equivocating about the reduction surgery when, during a routine exam, doctors found fibroids in her breasts and recommended removing the fibroids. She leapt at the chance to have the reduction surgery at the same time. "When it came that I had a recommendation from doctors to do it, I was incredibly grateful."

She felt overwhelming gratitude when her out-of-town friends gave her a birthday dinner at their home. Premier restaurateurs, they planned a beautiful meal that ended with readings and poems. She wept during the preparations and dinner, where she was showered with attention. "I didn't have that in my family. As an adult I've gotten the experience through friends. The first time I experienced that was in therapy. As old as I am, it's kind of opening doors of emotion and stuff that in healthy families kids would have had growing up and would have shared with the people they were given birth by."

She came to her birthday dinner with a new cut and highlights in her hair. "I had never, ever, ever, done anything or put anything on my hair." Her trendy, short, and lightened hair gave her a dramatic new look, yet because for so long she was perceived as the dependable, steadfast, "old maid" counselor, the reactions were tepid. Her always-ready chuckle bubbled when she recalls a coworker asking, "What's different about you?"

> THERE IS EXCITEMENT ABOUT NOT BEING OLD AND ABOUT BEING THIS AGE. TO HAVE THE BACKGROUND AND TO LEARN MORE AND EXPLORE WITH OUR MINDS MORE AND LOOK AT FRIENDS UNAFRAID AND WITH SOME KNOWLEDGE.
>
> —Peg Tappe

Fifty is freedom to this woman who has been a therapist since 1975 but whose own inner work has dealt with intense childhood traumas. "It's the threshold you walk across, that you have permission to be who you want to be, with openness to anything you want to do. Finally, I feel like I'm my own person. I'm beginning to explore who I want to be and what that encompasses."

She is considering a change in career. To all changes, she brings innocence and spirituality. Until she was forty-nine, she had never seen an ocean. When she scuba-dove for the first time among sharks, "It felt like we were in a fairyland . . . the sharks were so graceful, they did not look at all ferocious. I couldn't believe that I was underwater so close to that life form that has been around for millions of years . . . I now have this comprehension that the ocean is one of the earliest parts of the whole earth." Being there is "like meditating and praying."

That experience has given her clarity. "The challenge is to just sort through the excess until you see the essence of life and take that in so that your soul is healed and you can grow."

SHARON NELSON

Sharon Nelson's husband planned a fiftieth-birthday dinner for her at the Columbia Tower Club, which overlooks spectacular nighttime Seattle. Toasts were made, and Sharon gave a short thank-you speech. It was lovely by all accounts and suitable for a woman who was chair of the Washington State Utilities and Transportation Commission.

Yet what really spoke volumes about her was a quiet celebratory decision she had made months earlier—to leave her job. In 1997, she took a one-year sabbatical from a position she had held for twelve years. The position had capped a sterling career in public law that she could trace from Washington D.C. to Washington State.

When the sabbatical was over, she sprang a bigger surprise. She wasn't going back; in fact, she didn't have, or want, another job.

Originally, she had been prompted by a feeling that she wanted to find new challenges. The sabbatical solved practical problems: She could search for work without a conflict of interest and she could join her husband for three months' leave in Europe. What she discovered at the end of the year was that she had no desire to return to work.

"I had said, 'Okay, I'll just give myself a year.' But I didn't do what I'd hoped I'd get done that year." She had planned to fill the holes in her life created by her career: to go to museums and shows, to take golf lessons and gardening classes, to read and read more, to exercise daily.

What she *did* do whetted her appetite. Because of exercise, she became healthier and lost twelve pounds. She had thrown away the stress of a daily three-hour commute. At the end of the sabbatical she wanted more: more gardening, more time with family, more freedom, more health. What satisfied her more than space, was pace—a livable, breathable daily rhythm that suited her body and her psyche. "I just like the pace, being able to do what I want when I want."

She had faced the men's world, and she had faced mortality. Her father had died and she herself had two brushes with breast cancer. She was about to answer the question that had plagued her the last few years at work. "We've proved that we can work like men. So what have we proved?

"It was time to really slow down and smell the roses. It was the antidote to my crazy life, to get my hands dirty in the garden. My husband and I have a second home in San Juan Islands [off Washington State]. With my being free and with many four- and five-day weekends we just are communing with the eagles and otters."

Communing with nature was denied her from the time she graduated from college. Almost instantly, she was trudging on a steep treadmill. "When I entered law school the whole feminist consciousness came. We started from a handful of women in law school to becoming one-third of the class. We set out to prove something." The frontiers and opportunities and the responsibility to maintain the movement propelled her forward.

However, "as we went along, we weren't aware of what it cost us in terms of stress." Now her perspective has changed. "It was great fun; I really contributed, but at some expense to psyche and to relationships."

She is confident that she still contributes—she consults for businesses from home and she has joined a number of corporate boards—but in her own time and style. Her style now juxtaposes chatting with CEOs with running out to find tile samples to match paint chips.

All of this shows. At a recent conference, "I had six people ask me, 'Have you grown? You look taller.' The burdens have been lifted off my shoulders. I'm looking rested and standing up straight and looking taller—and at our age, we're supposed to be starting to shrink now!"

She admits there was a temporary void, a hankering for attention and power after leaving her job. But "the more I get away from it, the gladder I am to be away from it."

She is asked constantly to join boards, is offered jobs, and takes a certain amount of criticism from women friends who think she is not busy enough, or not productive. "What's productive? That's not the question. I still want to make a contribution." In truth, "the hard part isn't keeping busy, the hard part is enjoying your leisure. People keep searching you out. I tell my friends I'm liking my life. I don't need another high-powered, high-stress life.

"I stopped needing other people's approval. It is nice to give up an identity with a profession. You can settle into your own skin and be comfortable." She relishes simplicity. "I'm so much more present in every moment that I'm in."

VII Transition

Motorcycle Odyssey

STEVE WATSON
SEPTEMBER 1, 1941

$\int$ teve Watson made a six-week, seven-thousand-mile motorcycle odyssey for his fiftieth and came streaming home through a golden afternoon to a street crowded with neighbors clapping and lampposts flapping with yellow ribbons.

"It was the most incredible thing to come across the Golden Gate Bridge [San Francisco] and ride through the city and ride home."

The glorious welcome capped a journey of learning and change. He had been humbled by the ride through rural western and midwestern towns. He journeyed through soaring highs and deep lows. Exhilaration and loneliness both accompanied him. "I saw marvelous, wonderful things. It was a spectacular trip but I didn't get to share it in real time. One day I was fighting my way through a field of flowers and afterward I could not share it." At night he fought a profound loneliness as he tried to write in his journal.

He had expected to communicate with small-town folks, but they remained aloof from this stranger who lit on their town for a night on his spanking-new Harley-Davidson. On the occasions that he would linger for more than a day, he would succeed in engaging townsfolk in genuine talk. These uncommon moments brought home the realization that he was one with humanity.

"I've been a changed person. All of these people I met have the same ambitions, aspirations, difficulties, sorrows, pains, joys. Everyone had the same dreams—it didn't make a difference whether you were rich, poor, black, white, or green. The human experience was shared by all of us."

He had been swimming the corporate stream of ninety-hour weeks, Armani suits, Italian loafers, a Porsche, and a Rolex. "This trip really brought home to me in an incredible way that none of those things were important at all. I came to understand things that were more important—relationships and people and a beautiful sunrise."

Now, "I'm just as ambitious and work just as hard, but

the trip put an incredibly different perspective on things. Incredibly wealthy people have as much heartache. Incredibly poor people have as much joy."

Ambition and hard work were the cornerstones of his life. Raised in a "dirt poor farming family," he put himself

through school and graduated in 1967. "I escaped Iowa in my late twenties, and went to discover the world."

The same hunger for adventure that prompted him to dream of joining a circus converted to the energy that gobbled up career goals. He rose quickly in sales and marketing, eventually reaching management levels at a four-billion-dollar company. By 1984 he would sell the computer company he had formed and retire. Thereafter he lived independently, going in and out of retirement, consulting and investing.

He has been similarly hard-driven about adventuring. Since the '70s he has made a list of things to do. Each year, he adjusts it. It has included being in a circus, bungee jumping, skydiving, living in Paris for a year, living in Japan for three years. Airplanes, like motorcycles, have been a great love and aerobatics, barnstorming in old biplanes around the country, and flying a helicopter have been on his list. So was the odyssey by motorcycle.

It happened that he chose the odyssey just before his fiftieth, and yet, it seemed almost as if the adventure chose him at just the right time.

He began with typical, highly motivated, high-dreamer's energy. "I bought a brand-new Harley-Davidson with all the touring junk. I really went in style." He shipped the bike to Oshkosh, Wisconsin, in time for the town's annual air show, touted as the largest in the world, drawing one million attendees. His route would reach north into Canada, then wend down to California.

He also attended another gathering, the Sturgis Rally in South Dakota, the Annual Black Hills Classic. As it happened, it was the fiftieth anniversary of the rally and that year it drew an unprecedented number of attendees, 750,000. Serendipity had handed him some great milestones.

> I CAME TO UNDERSTAND THINGS THAT WERE MORE IMPORTANT: RELATIONSHIPS AND PEOPLE AND A BEAUTIFUL SUNRISE.
>
> —*Steve Watson*

He had set out on the journey with great goals. He told himself he would rediscover small-town U.S.A. and study its ability to survive.

He discovered, with sadness, that you can't go home again. "I had this fantasy that you can wander into the village bar and sit down with locals and discuss the meaning of life." But no, he remained an outsider.

"Each night I would find myself planning the next day's trip and I was not in a mood to write in my journal. I was filled with emotion and incapable of capturing it."

He found joy immersing himself in the greatness and smallness of natural beauty but a simultaneous sadness at being excluded from communicating its intimate lessons. "I was sitting by a stream and watching fish and chipmunks. In Montana, I saw an eagle. It was just a powerful thing to see God's creatures in that sort of unrestricted natural setting. We were all pretty equal."

That equality brought him to his senses as he crossed fifty. "Instead of choosing to accumulate, there was [from fifty on] the living to do."

He hopes to extricate himself from the load of business relationships to which he seems magnetically and inescapably drawn. Yet, "I'm back at it. I still love my toys, but I know they're not important in the grand scheme of things."

He continues to chase the adventures on his eternally young list. There are ones to cross off and ones to add each year, but he is realistic. Bungee jumping will probably come off. As for skydiving, he has probably another fifteen years to do that. In truth, "the issue is whether I live long enough to do all these things."

Standing in the Gambia River

PAM SHIPP

As the day approached, Pam Shipp's mantra had been "I don't want to be fat and fifty." She did eventually find fitness, but she was delivered in a deeper way. That year, she visited Africa for the first time. There, she found strength and a reason for being.

"It was magical. I felt so connected. Standing on the shores of the Gambia River [in Gambia] at Fort Myers, where slaves were stored and shipped off, was transforming. I had to return to my roots to get in touch with my purpose."

A licensed psychologist who works with people of color, she didn't know what she lacked until the water flowed before her. She realized then that the problems of African-Americans stemmed not from slavery alone. They included the scars of the passage from Africa to America.

In the aftermath of this experience, she was able to find pride: her people survived the uprooting. "It gives you something to be proud of—to go through that inhumanity of being stripped from your culture and then to survive that."

The feelings, like the river, coursed through her. "I was standing in that river, a Ph.D. woman. I thought, 'I come from a damn strong people.'"

She left with renewed strength to finish her work and to write about racial acculturation. "I have an understanding of oppression and of our place as African-Americans in society, and how to cope and to be happy."

Pam, left, with her mother in Gambia.

THEKLA SANFORD
NOVEMBER 3, 1946

*T*hekla Sanford always liked her parties big. Her November 3 birthday is strategically placed for celebratory outbreaks—it is often Election Day and close to the wildest, most hallowed of Mexican celebrations, the Day of the Dead.

Her celebrations have always been marked with creative generosity. She's thrown big Halloween parties where she gives out T-shirts drawn with skeletons, and election dinners in which each course parodied the presidential candidates. For her fortieth, she invited forty friends from her past, beginning with those from preschool, and took them to Mexico, putting them up in a hotel and giving them a five-day tour.

For her fiftieth, she was stumped. "I thought about

I WOULD NEVER THINK I
WAS FIFTY AND I WAS OLD.
THE ONLY THING THAT'S
ANNOYING IS GETTING
THIS AARP STUFF.

—*Thekla Sanford*

doing something else, but after my fortieth, what else could I do? I knew I couldn't repeat that."

As it turned out, she didn't want to. She tapped a different source within herself. "Forty was, like wild. This was more like an inner feeling—like I was looking inside myself," she reflected. "Now I wanted something quieter, just my husband and me. I thought of Oaxaca, Mexico. I'm much more at a place in my life now where the spiritual part of life is important to me. I just wanted to be in a place where I had a connection to bigger things."

Always connected to Mexico—she goes there every year—she gravitated toward Monte Albán, the pyramid ruins of the great Zapotec culture outside Oaxaca. From the time of her first visit to Monte Albán in 1986, to 1991, when she went for the total eclipse of the sun, she has felt "really safe and good to be there, almost like I'd been there before."

On the day of her birthday, her husband woke early, went to the Oaxaca market, and brought into their hotel room masses of flowers, filling the large space. He came in bearing a stunning, huge bundle of calla lilies and a large cross studded with flowers. It was a funeral cross.

"It was just beautiful. I laughed. I asked myself, 'Do I actually feel like I'm dying?'" She decided she was. "My daughter was turning eighteen. This is a cycle of my life, it is the end. So I was starting a whole new cycle."

Fifty in and of itself didn't bother her. "When my mother turned fifty, it was time to hunker down and grow old. You can get stuck in that and not grow at all. I was excited about being fifty. You just realize that women are excited that we know ourselves. I don't care about what people say, what people think. I don't care about any of that stuff anymore. I am going to be who I am. I'm still learning.

"Some people figure this out when they're thirty." However, at fifty "I have a lot of life . . . a lot of wisdom under my belt" to go with this independence. "I would never think I was fifty and I was old. The only thing that's annoying is getting this AARP stuff."

The rest of the day unfolded simply, rich in the smallness of its details—but not before she would be tested. A driver took them to a restaurant run by a family of sisters in nearby Teotitlan. A bottle of Sanford Winery Pinot Noir, one of their best wines made at the winery in the central Santa Barbara valley in California, accompanied the meal.

They then rode up the mountain and reached Monte Albán just as a group of tourists came streaming down. There, a guard announced that the mountaintop was closed.

She could not go up.

"I was just devastated. This was really important to me." Repeated appeals yielded nothing. Then, the driver, an old friend, took the guard aside and spoke to him. He came back to tell her that she had fifteen minutes to climb to the top. "This was something a lottery payola couldn't fix."

Minutes before five thirty-five, she was given the okay. "I walked and then I was running and I climbed up on a pyramid and took a lot of deep breaths, looking out. And exactly at my birth time, I turned around and there was a rainbow. It was absolutely beautiful. I started crying. I took it as a very good sign for the next fifty years. That moment, to be there, that it did work out, that we had to struggle to get in there, it meant a lot to me."

The rainbow filled a chasm that had opened before her. "My career is my wine business and raising my daughter was a big part of it. I took it very seriously. During her teenage years I gave up a lot. When I realized that she was leaving, I wondered where was I going, what to fill myself up with.

"The rainbow was there as support."

VIII Adventure

Leaping to Thailand

CHERI AND MIKE POTTER
AUGUST 12, 1946, AND MAY 21, 1944

*C*heri and Mike Potter took a blind leap at age fifty and, when they opened their eyes, found they had landed in paradise. Behind them in Oklahoma was a home, family, jobs, and retirement; and at their feet was Chiangmai, Thailand. The day they were offered jobs in Chiangmai, they accepted, then dashed breathlessly for their garage-sale globe. "We didn't even know what country Chiangmai was in," said Cheri.

There, they found themselves walking in a magic land. "In the States, I felt like I knew it all, but the rebirth process of moving into a completely different culture has changed me. We are like children living on sensory overload in Asia and our lives are so much richer over here," said Mike.

The two of them had accepted jobs at a Christian

school in up-country Thailand and saw their work as part mission, part adventure. Nonetheless, magic was present in every moment of their lives, in the happy, exhilarated love they express for each other, and even in the way they happened onto Chiangmai.

Like much else in midlife, their story unfolded at a deliberate pace. They laid the plans for their dream purposefully—although not without moments of doubt and humor. It involved various stages of planning, letting go, rethinking, getting things in order, and then . . . leaping. The result was no less magical, and they had the grace to recognize it instantaneously.

Both were born and bred in Oklahoma City, and unlike their peers, plumbed Europe for adventure and learning. "While most of our friends were saving for '67 Chevys, we were saving for a round-trip plane ticket to Europe," said Cheri. She was not a standard Oklahoma product. "My dad thought I had lost my mind when at age twenty-one, I announced I was going to Europe alone," she said in the singsong, dazzling-paced speech that seems still to belong to a twenty-one-year-old.

Mike, in the meantime, had toured Europe for three months by motorcycle.

IT REALLY IS THE BEST OF TIMES. MY KIDS ARE GROWN. I AM EMOTIONALLY, PROFESSIONALLY, AND FINANCIALLY FREE TO JUMP OFF THE CLIFF. I SEEM TO BE MORE WILLING TO TAKE THE RISKS ASSOCIATED WITH ATTEMPTING SOMETHING NEW AND UNKNOWN. I BELIEVE THAT IT IS NOT THAT THE ADVENTURE MAKES ME FEEL YOUNG AGAIN, IT'S THAT THE ADVENTURE HAS GIVEN ME A FULLER LIFE.

—*Cheri Potter*

The thirst for travel continued after they met and married. "So over the years, we began to talk about 'when the kids are gone—that's when we'd like to live overseas.'"

When Mike turned fifty and could soon collect teacher retirement benefits, "we began talking about it to our family." Cheri voluntarily retired when Mike did at age fifty-two. At fifty she found parting from security more painful than she imagined. She was walking away from sixteen years of "the job of a lifetime that I dearly loved," as student activities director for college kids. Dreaming up "wild and crazy programs" suited her garrulous, comedic style beautifully. "And they paid me to do this."

Her friends dared her to walk away from this work, and, indeed, her resignation felt like "that first step off a high cliff, down into the unknown. I knew there was no turning back. I swear I was a nervous wreck. I was convinced that we were nuts, that we weren't ready for this big a jump. I was so scared."

That fear turned into whoops and cheers the day they packed all their belongings after leading a summer camp for teenagers. "The day had been so stressed and hurried . . . we rounded a curve that we always loved for its beautiful view. Mike suddenly pulled over and we both got out . . . and laughed out loud and hollered, 'We did it.' That was when I knew we did the right thing."

Soon after, "we formulated the plan." They signed up for the Job Fair for International Teachers in early 1997. Mike prepared seventy résumés and sent them to

Egypt, Italy, Ireland, Scotland, Spain, England, Malaysia, Turkey, Dubai, Kuwait, Japan, Taiwan, Indonesia, and Thailand prior to the job fair. The fair quickly burst their bubble. Nobody hired them. "They mostly wanted young teaching couples." Shaken, Cheri intoned, "Well, so much for the old folks living overseas."

Then came the telephone call from the Chiangmai International School in Thailand. They didn't know what country Chiangmai was in, none of their friends did either, and many counseled them against this move.

Three months later, they landed in Thailand, having packed a shortwave radio and being prepared for the worst. "At least we could sit in our hut and listen to the BBC and Voice of America," said Mike. That was how much they knew about Thailand.

What they discovered was a charming and sophisticated civilization at once youthful and age-wise, with plenty to teach them. They didn't need a shortwave radio; in fact, they could not learn enough of what was in front of them. "One week in Thailand is like spending three months in Oklahoma. Everything is new and strange. The teacher in me wants to continue to learn. I am in the perfect place to do just that," said Mike.

They were fulfilling their dreams in another way—the "why" of wanting to live overseas. "We had been so blessed in our lives, it was a good time to pay back and help others," said Mike, who compares the teaching they do to missionary work.

The two are open about the length of their adventure in Thailand. They are paid in Thai currency, with just enough to live on. Yet, "It really is the best of times. My kids are grown. I am emotionally, professionally, and financially free to jump off the cliff. I seem to be more willing to take the risks associated with attempting something new and unknown. I believe that it is not that the adventure makes me feel young again, it's that the adventure has given me a fuller life," said Cheri.

She sums up their Asian adventure by paraphrasing a line from a James Taylor song: ". . . the secret of life is enjoying the passage of time . . . By retiring and setting out on our Asian adventure, we enhanced our lives and are enjoying our own passage of time, our fifties, much better than we would have if we had stayed safe and secure."

JACK KUSSMAUL

APRIL 2, 1942

J ack Kussmaul defied his surgeon's warning and ran the London Marathon to celebrate fifty.

Seven years earlier, after knee surgery, he had asked for the plain truth: Were there any limitations? The answer: "I don't think I'd be running marathons if I were you."

Being a lawyer and a realistic one, he knew the truth when he heard it. "Sure I could go elsewhere and pay for some new advice," but instead, he took up alternative activities, such as cross-country skiing and biking.

He didn't stop reading runners' magazines, however, and when he saw that an upcoming London Marathon would take place on April 12, he seized on it. "It was a great way to turn fifty, and what my surgeon doesn't know won't hurt him."

He trained with the wisdom of the nearly fifty years behind him. "I trained enough to get in shape but not enough to injure myself."

As he trained, some questions nagged him. His ongoing joke had been, "What, me having trouble about turning

fifty?" He admitted that "ego, challenge, and youth was all part of the mix" of marathoning. He also knew "I did want to prove to myself that I wasn't over the hill, but that wasn't the primary thing." What mattered to him was the celebratory experience.

ALL THE BUGS ARE WORKED OUT. AS LIFE GOES ON YOU ELIMINATE THE THINGS THAT DON'T WORK, YOU KNOW WHAT MAKES YOU HAPPY AND WHAT DOESN'T. THE ONLY PROBLEM IS THERE'S LESS AHEAD OF YOU.

—*Jack Kussmaul*

London delivered. He was doing something he had been advised to give up. Above all, he reveled in the city and the event itself. "People were out in front of pubs with beers, shouting. It was really festive. All along the route they wandered with boom boxes playing 'Proud Mary.'" Because of the festive bloom over the affair, he did not "hit the wall," a lag that marathon runners expect after completing twenty-four of the twenty-six miles, when all energy is depleted.

Finally, he celebrated the realization that "it would not be the last one. I would [still] run one occasionally."

What he gloried in was living itself. "At the last few miles . . . I was feeling exhilarated. I had done it. My knee, my back were fine. It all went gloriously." He had run his slowest time, but he no longer cared. He had given back to himself the gift of running, the "sense of my lungs feeling bigger than they've ever been before, feeling good for oneself, and in control of my life.

"I've never seen my doctor again."

Conquest of Italy

MAYA POOL

M aya Pool got out of bed at fifty and demanded more from life. "If this is all there is [to turning fifty], it's not enough. I asked myself, 'What do I really want to do? *Really* want to do—no limitations, no boundaries, nothing.'"

The answer flashed instantly. She would take her daughter to Italy. "I asked myself, 'Where do they really love children? Italy.' We would go to Florence, they're used to blond-haired English-speaking women there, and Italian men love blond women. Armed with these thoughts, I went to Europe."

She laid the groundwork. The single mom would put her estate in order, research lodgings, visit Italy and choose a residence, look over schools and horseback riding facilities, and set up for a year-long sojourn with her daughter. Before leaving, she had a face-lift and grew her hair long. Feeling gorgeous, she took off.

With her fifth-grade daughter dressed in American Gap, and herself in Armani and black heels, they set off first for London, then Greece and Istanbul. They landed

in Italy for a year filled with wonder. "It was fabulous. I looked thirty-eight. I had fifty years of experience and I was doing okay."

She found, "the community was wonderful. I had an incredi-

THIS IS THE OTHER SIDE OF THE LINE. ON THE ONE HAND, YOU'RE FACING DEATH. WHEREAS ON THE OTHER, YOU CAN SAY HOW RICH ARE YOU GOING TO MAKE THESE MOMENTS, THESE YEARS.

—Maya Pool

ble Italian lover and I never was not there for my daughter."

For her, the adventure confirmed her arrival on the scene of life. "I took myself with me and all the work I did on me and I found I had the tools for whatever situation came up." She had "found the stage and an audience" for herself. At fifty, "when we accumulate all these skills, we can suddenly bring it all into play."

> [FIFTY IS] KNOWING THAT WHEN SOMETHING IS RIGHT, THE ENERGY OF THE UNIVERSE GETS BEHIND YOU.
>
> —*Maya Pool*

If she had doubted she could take herself to a foreign country and support her daughter, the doubts vanished. "I don't think I made a bad decision for the whole year."

She and her daughter had time and space to learn about each other without the interruptions of child custody arrangements. "I had one continuous year with my daughter when I made the decisions. We had to depend on each other solely. We developed incredible trust in one another."

They learned that "two women can get along anywhere in the world. We learned how to go out and come back. The twisted streets of Italy were a metaphor for life."

She herself had accrued wisdom, foremost about intuition. "When something is right the energy of the universe gets behind you. With the decision to go to Italy, I had the energy of the universe behind me."

Finally, the trip gave her time to look back. "Italy is not about doing, it's about being. So I had a chance to reflect on who I had become." She liked the reflection. "I had become a woman with fifteen years of recovery. The promises of Alcoholics Anonymous were coming true in my life—that I would intuitively know what I know, that I would not close the door on the past but embrace it. All of it had brought me to this point and to deny it would be to deny me.

"It was such a gift."

Alive and Hang Gliding

PETER BIRREN

AUGUST 2, 1947

Peter Birren, veteran hang-glider pilot and passionate performer of twenty-three air shows, looked death in the eyeballs and survived a nose-dive crash on his fiftieth.

Three weeks later he was hang gliding again. Life was a choice and he would live it passionately. He would revel in an activity that at its most ordinary gave him extraordinary perspective, juxtaposing life and death and joy and pain. If anything, the accident heightened his appreciation of living and of his sport.

He had gone up, as he had for twenty-one years, on a normal, ordinary, good-weather weekend. "On my birthday, I made a bad decision because I ignored a judgment." He, who had logged thousands of air hours, had disregarded the reading of air currents and temperature just before takeoff.

As a result of the accident, he stopped chasing some records. "I'm more willing now to accept things for what they are." Almost immediately, however, some personal bests began rushing toward him. He set personal records for most flying days, most two-hour-plus flights, longest cross-country distance, and the most number of hours in the air.

He would let achievements come to him. "I'm fifty going on sixteen. If I

I HAVE A GREATER FEELING OF SELF-WORTH, OF PERSPECTIVE, OF MY PLACE IN THE WORLD. THERE ARE STILL THINGS I'D LIKE TO DO. NOW I HAVE THE PATIENCE TO KNOW I'LL GET TO THEM.

—*Peter Birren*

thought I could do something when I was twenty, now I should be able to do it . . . I have a greater feeling of self-worth, of perspective, of my place in the world. There are still things I'd like to do. Now I have the patience to know I'll get to them."

IX Power

KATHIE ROMINES

K athie Romines pursued her fiftieth birth-day as she has all projects in her life—she went after the best. Determined to outdo every other birthday celebration she's held, the self-made millionaire planned a trip to Italy for herself, her husband, and eight friends. In the span of a week, they would partake in the life of the Italian aristocratic families: they roamed their castles, sat as guests at their tables, tasted their wines, and dined on centuries-old porcelain and silver.

"It was a fairy tale. It was absolutely magical. We were kings and queens for a week."

The week began months earlier when she sent a teaser-poem to the invitees (see page 138).

At 1500 hours on June 3, 1997, all ten appeared at the

Spanish Steps. What her guests did not know was that Kathie had flown twice to New York City to plan the trip with a luxury and cultural tour services group. She gave strict orders about what she wanted, from naming the specific sights in Rome, planning the forays into Chianti, Siena, and Como, down to setting the pace of the trip.

"I wanted never to be bored for two minutes. I wanted us always in a program and when it was over with we would be hungry for more." The command was in many ways her personal mantra.

Born in a small midwestern farm town of ten thousand, she rode the crest of opportunity. The compact, svelte woman, who dresses in sophisticated neutral tones and designer lines, is polished to the last strand of her perfect coif. She glides through the truck stop that she and her husband have built into a multimillion-dollar family business. It, too, is outfitted to the nines, a cutting-edge American entertainment and service center that, like her, looks to have outgrown its small-town surroundings. The restaurant seats 250 in beveled glass and wallpapered splendor, and includes an arcade of vintage puppets, showers and services for drivers, an in-house bakery, and decorations that change seasonally, like the menus. The center attracts not only

Kathie's turning '50'
Oh what will she do!!
She'll plan an exciting trip
And invite her favorite friends — You!!

We'll meet at the top
Of the Spanish Steps in Rome
And tour the majestic sights
Which the Gladiators once called home

After a visit to St. Peters
And the Sistine Chapel too
We are off to explore
A medieval castle or two

At gourmet restaurants in Tuscany
We will exquisitely dine
Tour the Chianti Vineyards
For a glass or two or three of wine

Beautiful frescoes in ancient churches
And Michelangelo's grand work of art
Will be just some of the glorious sights
That will remain in our minds and heart

Beautiful Lake Como will enchant us
With its tranquillity and grace
Golfing and lake boat rides
Will pick up the pace

Until the very last minute . . . and second
We will continue to celebrate in Style
For Kathie will only be 50
For just a little while

So come, join in the Celebration
She wants you all to be there
To remember this Special occasion
And the excitement and fun we will share

SPECIAL PEOPLE & PLACES THAT YOU WILL ENCOUNTER ON KATHIE'S BIRTHDAY BASH ITALY, JUNE 1997

YOUR HOST & TRIP ESCORT
Marina Dalle Rose:
Her father descends from one of
that gave to the city three Doge
Her mother belongs to the Rica
Chianti. She studied to be a si
and Spanish and has worked i
Relations. She also organized
Italian companies. She has sp
managing her mother's estate
(unfortunately not wine) Sh
as her interest has always be

GUIDE IN ROME
Margherita Olberg-Guid
She graduated at the U
being on Baroque Art.

Kathie's Birthday Bash

TUESDAY JUNE 3: ROME

Morning:
Individual arrivals into Rome,
(Suggest: Airport Taxi-Lire 80,000-luggage included).
Proceed on your own to the hotel Intercontinental De
La Ville.
One of Rome's finest traditional hotels on the top of
the Spanish steps.

1500
Meet at the top of the Spanish Steps, or, if it is rain-
ing, in the lobby of the hotel. Also meet your special
tour escort & Italy host Marina Dona Dalle Rose.

1500-1930
Proceed on a half day tour with your special guide
Margherita Olberg. Visit the Roman sites, the Church
of San Clemente, Michelangelo's Moses in the
Church of San Pietro in Vincoli, Piazza Navona and
Fontana di Trevi. Bring binoculars.

truckers but a growing population of families in search of entertainment. Ever pushing for growth, she is projecting a hotel and conference center on the site.

This former farm girl took the greatest advantage of the feminist revolution and knows it.

"The best thing of being fifty years old is I'm glad I'm not forty, I'm glad I'm not sixty. It's fabulous. We're on the precipice of the women's movement," she said, nibbling dry toast and sipping black coffee in the restaurant as dishes of bacon and eggs and waffles topped with swirling cream swoop by on waitresses arms.

By staying in a small town, she could better appreciate the gains of the feminist revolution. When she grew up, "There wasn't even a lady policeman. It's so fabulous to watch what I've watched in the last thirty years. My sixty-year-old friends didn't have the edge that the fifty-year-olds have. The forty-year-olds will never experience the excitement and thrill we had."

Married in 1968 soon after she finished high school, she chose to be childless. Her business came first. She and her husband built their business around a small gas station he leased. They worked without a break for the first five years.

The division of labor in the marriage delineates itself clearly. "My husband is the dealmaker and I follow behind and make the deals work." She has no delusions about her contribution.

She also entertains no illusions about the world of power and men. To succeed, one must accept it. "We are still governed by the men's world." She lets loose a diatribe only for Hillary Clinton, who tried to compete with men on men's turf. "I feel she let us down. She couldn't do what she wanted on the male side. She got so mad that she stuck her hands in her pockets. What has she accomplished? She just won't give in [to the men's world]."

Success is achieved and frontiers taken by women with hard work and a true assessment of power. A woman should mind the boundaries in society and politics, but within her own life, she should grab power. "You have to give yourself your own power. And so we use the birthday as an example." We learn to give birthdays from our mothers, but women forget to use their own power to celebrate themselves.

Similarly, while she made sure her guests were pampered and were entertained endlessly for her fiftieth, she had also made certain she would enjoy the magic, too. "I bought the surprise for myself; I bought the package. Normally I'm the one who arranges trips. This was a reward to myself."

In nine breathless days, "Kathie's Birthday Bash" took in Rome, Chianti, Siena, and Como, where the ten were escorted by personal hosts of impeccable Italian lineage,

Kathie (front row, fourth from left).

stayed in private villas, and talked to descendants of great olive oil, wine, and cheese producers.

Each night, whether it was in a Tuscan stone village turned into a hotel or at the Villa D'Este, lovely mementos of the day—olive oil, hand-painted postcards—awaited each member of the party in their hotel rooms.

On the last night of the trip, they celebrated with a birthday dinner. She had asked that any gifts be created by the givers, not bought. She received poems, art, histories, and in the finale, a skit. In the skit, the Kathie character was on the phone doing what she does best—outdoing herself. She was pounding the desk and demanding "the best seats on the airplane." On her desk was a book, *The Best Hotels in the Universe*.

> BEING FIFTY IS ABOUT THE BEST TIME FOR ANYBODY WHO'S CAREER-DRIVEN.
>
> —*Kathie Romines*

As the skit performer said, "Kathie creates her own memories."

Perspectives from a Hot-Air Balloon

KAREN CARLSON

APRIL 22, 1943

aren Carlson's friends gave her a hot-air balloon ride to celebrate her fiftieth. It suited her idea of self at fifty. "Doing something adventurous speaks to the notion that growing older is not doing less and sticking with that which is familiar. It is to try out new things and go to new heights."

It was the perfect metaphor for perspective. She describes the ride: "It was very quiet, there's not much sensation of wind; you're moving with wind, you *are* the wind. Sometimes you touch down on treetops and you can pluck a leaf."

The overview given by the ride resonated with a sense of power that women of this age can have.

THE REAL MILESTONES ARE THE THINGS WE ACHIEVE.
—*Karen Carlson*

"It strikes me how fun it is to grow older. I work with young graduate students and I see these young women in their early twenties and I think of the kinds of stresses and tensions in their lives that are not in mine. It's so easy to let things go." She adds, "Growing older is not a sense of loss but a sense of accumulation of all you are and of learning more and focusing more. You have the opportunity to be more powerful rather than less."

Four-City Triumph

MARY FURLONG

OCTOBER 6, 1948

ounder and CEO of Third Age Media, and very much a woman of the '90s, Mary Furlong celebrated in four cities throughout the week of her birthday.

"I don't think we live in a community anymore with all our friends in one place and so I couldn't really have a party in one place. I have wonderful friendships in all those places."

The parties included a San Francisco sailing party for which her friends hired a Tom Jones impersonator, dinners in New York and Washington D.C., and a dinner in her hometown of Lafayette, California, with girlhood friends.

Among the gifts she received, appropriate for an editor with a vision: the twelve issues of *Life* magazine from 1948

147

and a copy of *Seventeen* magazine from the year she was seventeen. Her friends also hosted a Web site that displayed pictures of her throughout her life.

A faculty member at the University of San Francisco, she took a sabbatical to start Third Age Media, dedicated to those forty-five and over. Long recognized as a visionary on aging as well as on the Web, she left her position as a professor of education and technology to devote herself full time to the transition of the baby-boomer generation. In 1986 she founded the nonprofit SeniorNet, bringing computers to seniors. Now, her vision is to make it easy for third-agers to express themselves.

> IT'S ALL ABOUT CREATING YOUR OWN NEXT PATH.
>
> —*Mary Furlong*

"This generation is very different from what we've been thought of before. We're all about aspiration and entitlement." Baby boomers, she said, "want all the things they had when they were young. There's more of a sense of urgency. The clock is ticking. They want to make the most of the time—traveling, quitting jobs and starting over, getting divorced, doing thrilling things, things that are important to them."

As a woman on the forefront of change, of predicting

and branding the generation, she is writing as many books as possible to assist third-agers. Her publishing company has published a series of books, including *Computers for Kids over Sixty*. She writes a column, "Web for Grown-Ups."

She predicts that this generation will receive increasingly more e-mails on its birthdays than cards. One of her own favorite e-mails, which she received on her fiftieth, was this: "Turn the page—it's only going to get better ahead."

She will continue to live one of the phrases that she coined for Third Age. "It's all about creating your own next path."

IT'S A BIG DAY. IT'S LIKE SIXTEEN AND TWENTY-ONE. IT'S A DAY FOR GIFTS OF MEANING AND LASTING VALUE.

—*Mary Furlong*

NANCY SHAPIRO
FEBRUARY 3, 1947

N ancy Shapiro, silversmith and jeweler, sidestepped glitter and sought barren solitude for her fiftieth. She wanted isolation.

"I really wanted a deserted island, but I couldn't get to one so I headed for this fishing village in Mexico." For the thirty days surrounding her fiftieth, she lived by the sea and walked the sands. It was time to become like the sand, to sift and filter what the waves were throwing on shore. She was feeling engulfed and sullied. At fifty, she had to refine her own power and authority. When she emerged she had distilled what was precious and powerful.

Formerly a college metalsmith instructor, she moved to New Mexico in 1994 with her husband. Her teaching career over, she planned to continue her jewelry apparel business. She found herself involved in the Indian reservations around Taos. One of the pueblos asked her to teach silversmithing and she agreed because she had always taught and because she had always responded to the disadvantaged.

The result was life changing. "I probably got a bigger education for what teaching means in the pueblo than I did anywhere else." She had never taught students who were as hungry to learn; she had never had students who were so scarred.

However, after working with at-risk youths, she was "saturated." The poverty of reservation life and its futility, as well as the riches of its spirit life and beauty, were affecting her profoundly. "After two years I had come out on the other side between the magic and tragedy. My emotions ran the gamut daily. I was emotionally cooked."

In the meantime, she had also begun stuttering. She learned it was one of the symptoms of metal poisoning, or what is commonly called Mad Hatter's Disease. Depression and inclination to suicide can result from the disease. Silversmiths solder using cadmium, and after a lifetime of teaching and making jewelry, she had overloaded her system with the toxic metal.

Francois Robert

"All that was just shaking out of my system" at the same time that the pueblo-related emotions were spilling over. Stories of child abuse, spousal abuse, alcohol and drug abuse, and poverty had pelted her ears daily. "After a day was over, it felt like a year."

She headed for isolation.

On her birthday, she clarified her thoughts. "I was walking along the beach and looking at what I'd done." She realized that instead of quitting programs at the reservation, she would move on to the next stage. She could distill power and contribute from a distance. "The hands-on stage had passed by, but I did not give it up. I devised ways for money to continue in the pueblos. I'm not letting the links for success break."

Back from her retreat, she convinced a national corporation to donate twenty-five thousand dollars to the reservations for the apprentice and career program she had started. As well, she applied for and received federal grants for a fully equipped jewelry workshop.

For herself, she detoxicated and cleansed herself, using an herbal treatment. "When you're older you can't abuse yourself like you do when you're young. Now I see what it takes to take care of yourself. I'm counting my lucky stars that I'm coming through toxicity with no permanent damage."

She had distilled her knowledge and purified her own energy as an artisan. Rather than risk her health further by using silver she turned to gold. At three hundred dollars an ounce, buying gold meant a commitment to her own worth as an artist. Silver is three dollars a pound. She took the leap. "I realized that my own skill level is such that there's no reason not to do this work in gold." Her essence, she now knew, was in herself.

x Purpose

HOWARD SHAPIRO

FEBRUARY 7, 1947

On his birthday, Howard Shapiro found acceptance.

He had left behind in New Mexico his farm and beloved gardens, and trekked to New York City. There he made an impassioned speech before editors at Bantam Books about his manuscript, *Gardening for the Future of the Earth*. To his complete joy and some surprise, they understood. They accepted his manuscript for publication.

"It was the day I had my epiphany with my editors. You put your ass on the line, and all of a sudden they go, 'I got it.'"

He was grateful for the challenge. "Something I thought was important was accepted by people who by nature need to doubt what you were saying. We engaged in

Francois Robert

MY BEARD IS COMPLETELY WHITE
AND MY HAIR HAS CHANGED
POSITIONS ON MY HEAD BUT
EVERYONE SAYS I HAVEN'T CHANGED.
EVERY DAY I WORK AS HARD AS I
WORKED THE DAY BEFORE AS SOON
AS I START TO WORK.

—*Howard Shapiro*

a very profound dialogue. For that I'm forever thankful. They made me make it understandable."

The book realized his own dream—to proclaim a revolution in agricultural practices from the bottom up, "so when you step out of the doorway, you know which way the wind blows and how to save water. It teaches you to make decisions about a window garden to a backyard garden to a community garden, and how to influence the ecosystem. Pretty soon you're giving seeds to a neighbor and pretty soon, you have plenty of trees and you're giving tomatoes to them." Suddenly, one's community can become like paradise.

"Gardening is where paradise is found. The word *paradise*

comes from two Middle Eastern words meaning a walled hunting garden, a place where everything was found."

The force of the truth struck him. "I realized that day that it was true, and Bantam got it." He had found power in the peaceful method of uncovering truth, a real revolution. "I provide people with options in the book, not lambs to slaughter."

The radical gardener and pioneer of biodiversity and organic systems has traveled an impassioned road in his personal life. A radical student of the '60s who received a Ford Foundation grant to work in African-American communities in the Deep South, he then became an artist and ceramist. Afterward, he taught college art. During that period, he also became publisher of the leftist *New Art Examiner*.

During these art and social justice years, he was all the time observing gardening and food production systems in the American South, in Europe, and in Asia. As well, he was rooted in the practices of his Eastern European immigrant parents who were "so determined to have gardens that fed them."

Conviction eventually pressed him to leave the prestigious teaching job. In the early 1990s, he took a leap of faith and joined Seeds of Change, an organic seed company based in New Mexico. He is currently its vice president of agriculture.

"To write this book was a response to all those years of looking. This dream actually turned out. It wasn't modest in its intention. We're talking about the best system for food production. Besides clean air and water, there's nothing more important for our planet."

To research, he traveled to the radical practitioners and scientists around the world who were sounding a clarion call to change production practices that poison the earth and deplete it of nutrients. He compiled their theories. "I saw what these characters went through to do these things and that they were geniuses and I could consolidate [their principles]."

Rather than attack corporate agriculture, he challenges and invites comment: "Can anyone say anything more?"

His departure from art to gardening has not been radical, however. "My world is plants and biodiversity. What I see leaves me with total wonderment and makes me feel so small. I marvel at the painterliness of the whole thing. Wherever I go I see the waves of flowers move with the wind. You see swatches of [plant] color whether it is in downtown Los Angeles, Bolivia, Brazil, or China."

On the evening of his birthday, after his impassioned plea, he found himself at a table in a New York restaurant with a community of believers: his editor, his coauthor, company associates, and his oldest friend. He felt grateful and purposeful.

"I was both exalted and very somber. When people take you seriously, it is sobering. Joy has many faces."

THIS THRESHOLD MAKES PEOPLE TAKE YOU MORE SERIOUSLY. IT'S OUR PROUD MOMENT. IT'S BEING ABLE TO SYNTHESIZE EVERYTHING WE'VE LOOKED AT FOR THIRTY YEARS.

—*Howard Shapiro*

Return to Africa

HARRY WILLIAMS

OCTOBER 2, 1948

As he prepared to turn fifty, Harry Williams's life took some surprising twists. He swerved past mortality a few times, but in the end he used the experiences to create a legacy.

The college history professor began with a goal of going to Africa at fifty. Before he could go, however, he discovered he had diabetes. He reacted with, "Oh my God, I may not live to be fifty." All the same, when he had his condition under control and he had become healthier in the process, he did travel to Ghana.

He savored the trip for the personal victory that it represented and for the expanding identity he received as a person of African descent. "As my birthday approached I became even more concerned about the question of legacy."

In the most cruel twist of all, the three most important women in his life had died only recently. His mother, his grandmother, and his great-aunt. His mother was responsible for keeping him in school; his grandmother for keeping him in church; and his great-aunt for taking him to Broadway shows.

"As a way of showing my gratitude to them and to work through my grief, and as a way of demonstrating, in a proactive way, support for academic excellence, I decided to establish a prize."

He grew up in "Jim Crow, Richmond [Virginia]" and went to a segregated high school. "A tradition was to drop out and go to work. Many guys in my neighborhood dropped out." Unlike today's dropouts, they "hustled and got jobs." But he was encouraged to continue in school by these women. "If there was a kind of love and caring and steadying hand, it was theirs. Without them I probably would have become a street boy and probably wouldn't have been as successful as I am now."

While he was discussing the establishment of the Williams/Harris Prize in African-American Studies, he had been told gently by development officials at Carleton College, where he taught, that as a donor, it was customary to make a 50 percent financial commitment to the endowment. "I swallowed," said the 6-foot-3-inch, 295-pound professor, shaken even by the memory. "I would have to put up ten thousand dollars. I assure you I am not a rich man." At about the same time, his colleagues wanted to give him a party. When they learned about the prize, they turned the party into a benefit.

The party did make him feel a rich man. While he pledged two thousand dollars a year for five years to create the endowment, his friends contributed eight thousand dollars. "It was really classy. A jazz band played. There were 100, 150 people," he said. "It was a wonderful party, a great way to turn fifty."

JOSIE NATORI

Josie Natori took care of three anniversaries with one extravagant, determined celebration: her fiftieth birthday, her twenty-fifth wedding anniversary, and the twentieth anniversary of her firm. To do that, she rented Carnegie Hall, moved her piano there, invited 2,800 guests, hired an orchestra, and gave a concert as the soloist. The New York society pages buzzed with the event.

At the heart of the concert, however, was not a big-bang display but the realization of a dream. A child prodigy in the Philippines, she had begun playing at age four. This concert, more than forty years later, stood as a mark of love for her husband and family, and also for herself and music.

Playing live before an audience is "something to do at twenty; it's another to do it at fifty. It's a different stage of life and it's wonderful to do something I love. I love music but I didn't give it the devotion I would have liked. Now I had the occasion to do it."

On the evening of May 20, the powerful and petite designer and president of House of Natori walked onto the stage of Carnegie Hall, and, backed by an eighty-five-piece orchestra, played the Schumann Piano Concerto in A minor and the Rachmaninoff Piano Concerto No. 2, two of the most difficult in the piano repertory. In the front of the house sat her family, school friends, associates from the finance world and the fashion industry.

"It just became an opportunity to do something. Over the years, it became a goal for myself to do something different." The last concert she gave was at age nineteen, yet "all the time I knew I loved playing the piano and I would go back. It was a nice gift to my husband."

She prepared for three years. Over those years, the event grew. At first she thought she would play a movement of a concerto, then it became the entire concerto, then another concerto was added. The guest list also mushroomed. When a documentary about her planned performance was aired, "it became more public than I wanted. I couldn't turn my back."

She faced the situation with the same determination and

élan that put her onstage in the Philippines as a child, that put her in this country as a teenager, on Wall Street as vice president of Bache Securities, and then in a position to start her own business. The woman who heads a twenty-five-million-dollar empire didn't back down. For two years she practiced daily as soon as she reached home from work and for six hours a day on weekends. She didn't go to her country house more than five times in the two years before the performance.

Like many who achieve great goals, she didn't feel pressure so much as she was spurred by the challenge. "Running a business and practicing wasn't compatible. It was a question of fitting it in." She harnessed certitude. "I knew the time was coming and I wasn't going to falter."

Playing a concert at fifty in some ways aptly summed up herself and music. "This event has forced me to be better and to play for myself. When I was young, I had to go through [performing]. Now, it's because I want to. When you turn fifty, you want to."

XI Community

Surprise Chocolate Buffet

LOUISE LECHNER

JULY 11, 1948

Louise Lechner's birthday was a love fest for the women in her group, friends that met poolside as pregnant mothers-to-be.

For previous birthdays, "we bought each other a lot of jewelry over the years, and we'd chip in if something was expensive," said Louise. As they began to turn fifty, one woman celebrated by inviting the seven to a mountain cabin. Another held a big bash around Fiesta, the mammoth three-hundred-year-old religious festival of Santa Fe, New Mexico.

When it came to her, Louise, who is a weaver and runs a gallery, realized, "for my fiftieth I didn't need anything except more yarn." She decided to ask the group for contributions to her newfound volunteer activity—teaching intergenerational knitting at a teen center. The center had just lost funding from the National Endowment for the Arts. She realized that money and backing were an ongoing need for those in the group: women in their sixties, teens, and elementary school children who were making a knitting circle weekly at a local teen center. It had moved her that through learning a traditional skill, the women were communicating with and supporting each other.

Suddenly it occurred to her that "rather than get a couple of hundred dollars [from her close friends], I could get several thousand" if she turned to a bigger community.

She created an announcement on red card stock. "Facing Fifty Fearlessly" included a pencil drawing of a woman with hair standing up. On the border were the messages to eat more chocolate, to support art, and to celebrate her birthday by sending a donation to the teen center. To her lunch group friends, she gave firm instructions: Don't give me anything; donate to the center. With that, she was content, Amen.

Her lunch group, however, was not content. If Louise had enlarged her thinking about fund-raising, they would better her. On the sly, they expanded the fund-raiser list and invited friends from Louise's past to a surprise party, a

June 23, 1998

Dear Friends:

Please join us for a Surprise 50th Birthday party for Louise Lechner. Our local fashion maven, talented weaver, and dear friend Louise will celebrate her 50th birthday on July 11th. In her true style, she announced at a recent lunch that this year rather than gifts, she would like her friends to make a small contribution to the SF Teen Arts Center Warehouse 21 where she volunteers her time teaching knitting. We booed and hissed and told her she was no fun, but in the end we understood how committed she is to this cause. So we agreed. NO gifts! But . . .

She didn't say we shouldn't have a party! So if Louise has touched your life as she has ours, please join us on Thursday evening, July 9 slightly before six at the Teen Arts Center Warehouse 21, 1614 Paseo de Peralta for a "Nothing but Chocolate Buffet." Tom will be bringing her by about six, so please arrive a little early!

Our dream is to present a sizeable check to Warehouse 21 in honor of Louise on her 50th from all of her friends. If you would like to participate, just place a donation in the gift box we will have at the door. If you cannot attend, but would like to contribute and be listed on our card to Louise, send a check to:

Ana Gallegos y Reinhardt
Santa Fe Teen Arts Center, Warehouse 21
1614 Paseo de Peralta
Santa Fe, NM 87501
We hope to see you there!

Sincerely,

The Ladies who lunch with Louise!
(Penny, Annie, Diane, Maya, Marilyn, Judy, Ceil, & JB)

Regrets only: 983-1849

"Nothing but Chocolate Buffet."

"It was a stinking, rotten, dirty trick. If I could have run I would have. I felt like a deer," said Louise of the night she walked into the teen center and found herself the subject of a large party. Yet, as she went around the room and hugged each guest, she was rewarded with mem-

ories. "I visualized something we had done that had been a wonderful memory. It reminds you how rich your life was."

There was more. One of the luncheon group gave a speech. Besides Louise, she honored the group itself.

"We were all pregnant together thirteen years ago this summer; we started lunching together then and we have been consistent for thirteen years. We have come to lean on, honor, and respect each other. We're very different and none is perfect. We have learned about forgiveness, acceptance, courage, faith, gentleness. We've been through financial ups and downs, illness, deaths of parents, challenges of raising teenagers . . . and supported each other through all . . ."

Then she proceeded to introduce each woman; she concluded, "We are better at fifty than we were at thirty-seven."

LIFE RIGHT NOW IS VERY NICE. ALL I ASK IS TO HAVE AS MANY YEARS OF THIS AS I CAN HAVE. PHYSICALLY, YOU CAN'T FALL AND TURN AROUND AND GET RIGHT UP. MENTALLY, WE'RE MUCH MORE RESILIENT.

—*Louise Lechner*

Croning by Demand

TERRY TIPTON

*T*erry Tipton belonged in a group that originally had come together for support as stepmothers but remained friends after the children were grown. She turned to the group when year fifty approached.

Never one to hold back, she demanded a croning ceremony from them. "I thought turning fifty and menopausal in one year was adding insult to injury. I thought, 'If I have to do this I want a ceremony.'"

The divorced woman skimmed over a magazine story about croning just enough to know she wanted it. "I wanted to go into the positive aspects of being a woman. I had never done well for my birthdays, but I decided to celebrate. I made up my mind the more I said I was fifty it

173

would be easier. I celebrated the whole week by going out dancing a lot and I told everybody. Then everybody would buy me a drink and wish me happy birthday."

Meanwhile, her friends scrambled to learn about croning. Eventually, they created a ceremony. Fumbling, they culled from books on women and on the experiences of one of them who belonged to a women's spiritual group at a Unitarian church. They ended up with a ritual that none would forget.

It started on an evening after some typical "girl activities," but only after shooing Terry away as they improvised last-minute details. They ate pizza and watched one of their daughters' film about Appalachian mothers and daughters.

Then began the ritual. Its three parts were connected to natural elements—earth, water, fire. The concluding segment was a welcome into the circle. The hostess used the symbols for the ceremony as decorations.

First, she invoked the sunflowers in the centerpiece. They symbolized earth, she said, giving the largest to Terry. The smaller surrounding flowers were still vividly yellow, full and upright, but Terry's was drying out—it represented the passage into another phase, that of becoming useful.

Second, each woman told a story about an object she

had brought. The object belonged to a heroic woman in the storyteller's past. As each told her story, she poured water from a pitcher into a bowl, to symbolize blending the stories of womanhood. Then, each read or recited a passage. "Someone read from the Bible, another a poem about wearing purple . . ." said Terry.

Third, to represent fire, candles were lit. Each woman described herself before menopause and after menopause, addressing the pleasures of postmenopausal life. Fire symbolized what each had gone through in the crossing to cronehood. Each woman touched Terry's candle with the flame of her candle.

Finally, they presented Terry with a rose to welcome her into cronehood.

Outside of the ceremony, hormonal therapy had given Terry renewed vigor. "I'm more into what I look like; I get pedicures and massages. I'm interested in dating. So I keep up. I probably look better. I look even now ten years younger than when I was married. I have time for myself. I meditate."

The ceremony's effect was to transform the group. Said the organizer, "We were already so close, it brought us closer."

DAN AND
GEORGIA GOOCH

AUGUST 13, 1948, AND AUGUST 26, 1948

*E*arly in the summer of 1998, Dan and
Georgia Gooch sent out a teaser to some
100 friends and family—"we are planning a one-hundredth
birthday party." The number 100 was cheeky but held a
hidden significance.

Their Sunday afternoon family reunion was an elegant
event hosted in a restaurant. Nieces and nephews scam-
pered afoot, and relatives, friends, and associates shared
tables. A jazz band played and all danced. The only relatives not present were three parents. All had died long
before age fifty. The playful exaggeration around the number 100 meant something deeper to the two, who had chosen to be childless. As Georgia put it, "we never spoke it

176

out loud to each other, but it was saying that we had both made it."

June, 1998

Dear Family and Friends,

This year of 1998 finds the Gooches, both Dan and Georgia, turning 50. Appropriately these birthdays will be taking place at summer's end.

What we want to do is CELEBRATE the event with as many of our family members and friends as we can possibly gather.

To that end, we are announcing, at the beginning of summer, that we are planning a 100th BIRTHDAY PARTY celebration at the end of the summer.

We have reserved one of our favorite restaurants in Chicago; ZINFANDEL and one of the best and most eclectic musical groups will be the back drop for a party on the afternoon of Sunday, September 6, Labor Day weekend.

We'll be sending you a formal invitation closer to the date of the party. We just wanted you to know about our plans so that you could make your plans for what is usually a pretty busy weekend.

Dan and Georgia

DONN AND FRAN PEARLMAN

MAY 2, 1946, AND APRIL 4, 1946

*T*he Pearlmans had vacationed in Las Vegas since the '70s and five years before they both turned fifty, they had joked, "Let's have a party in Las Vegas for our fiftieth."

By February of 1996, fantasy had become fact. They made a straightforward offer to friends and family: Come and "we'll feed you for a couple of days."

All leapt at the chance, making their own hotel and air reservations and following instructions—no gifts. "We wanted just their presence but not their presents," said Donn.

Altogether twenty-four showed up Saturday night at an Italian restaurant for the simple reunion. Fifty, said Donn, is "one of those life events that you want to celebrate with family and close friends."

Bed-and-Breakfast Gathering

JIM WHEELER

It was a night for family and a repossession of childhood for a generation sandwiched between two. The simple get-together that Betsie Wheeler arranged for her husband became a sweet milestone for his entire family.

Timing was paramount. The children were grown and gone. So Betsie invited her in-laws to a bed-and-breakfast. For the first time in more than forty years, they were together under one roof.

"It was deeply moving. It was the most meaningful time I've had with my family for many, many years," said Jim. In this one night, conversations were uninterrupted, thoughts completed, and "You knew you were going to see each other at breakfast."

The last time the Wheelers were together was just before Jim's older sister, Martha Jane, married and left home. He was nine then. With Jim, the baby, turning fifty, it was the last of the generation reaching that milestone. That night, they crammed themselves into a limousine to go to dinner, came back to the B&B, and played bingo surrounded by vintage photographs.

"It got us to thinking about the history of our family. We were reminiscing and stories would come out that weren't funny then but were funny now," said Jim. Above all, his eighty-one-year-old mother could talk to her assembled children about their father, who died in 1971.

Normal Wheeler family reunions or Sunday get-togethers are noisy and crowded. Children and work schedules and just the sheer volume of people dilute interaction, Jim said. But their interaction that night was direct though never heavy. "Everyone brought something goofy and wrapped it up as bingo prizes," Betsie said. Among the gifts were five pounds of duck guano (poop), and Dracula wigs. "There are a lot of bald guys in the family, you see."

It was lighthearted, and soon stories, like jokes, started to build steam. As the stories spun out, sharing and forgiving took place. Some leaked tales that had not been heard before. For example, the one about the time that Jim's sister, Martha Jane, baby-sat two sick brothers. They battled that night over the merits of their coloring books. When the comparing, carping, and whining would not stop, Martha Jane walked into the boys' bedroom and in an attempt to equalize, ripped off the cover of Jim's book. On Jim's fiftieth birthday, Martha Jane gave him a coloring book.

"Everyone laughed a lot," said Betsie. Beyond that, everyone left refreshed and renewed because "some of the family was in need of getting away." A few in the group had recently put parents in nursing homes.

It was a tender, fragile moment, fraught with the sense of catching time and sweetness under one roof for one more time.

XII Commitment

JODI TAYLOR

AUGUST 29, 1947

When six middle-aged folks appeared for a whitewater rafting trip in the Grand Canyon, the guides relaxed: This was going to be a cruise. They were wrong. Instead, Jodi Taylor's birthday party would be the opposite of a placid boat ride for seniors. They chose to go the rapids on a small raft, and they would face-off death during a day in which friendship and commitment were as solid as the rock that surrounded them. The trip became a continuing celebration of herself and her friends.

She approached her birthday with ecstatic hope. "I saw turning fifty as a real celebration of life. Instead of seeing it as a milestone of aging I saw it as a milestone of how wonderful life can be," said Jodi Taylor, who had fought off breast cancer twice.

To start with, "It was an unbelievable bonding, spiritual experience. That five people whom I love would take nine days out of their busy schedule to celebrate with me was incredible," she said. As soon as she had called them, each friend said yes.

Second, "It was a celebration of love and commitment." The six—four friends of Jodi and her husband, ranging from forty-five to sixty-two—chose to go downriver in a small, rubber paddle boat on a day that the rapids were classified as extremely dangerous. Only later would she realize the meaning of their choice. "We got in the boat because of our commitment to each other. There was never a question of whether we would ever do it. We said, 'We're going to make this work.'"

As they went through the rapids, the accompanying kitchen boat capsized. "It was smashed to smithereens." Then, the paddle boat itself capsized. Yet her crew rescued the contents of the kitchen boat and continued. Later they learned that had they not recovered the kitchen equipment, the guide would have radioed for helicopter rescue.

She lived an eternity of feelings. "I was feeling incredibly responsible" for her friends when they chose the more dangerous course. It flashed through her mind, "You've survived breast cancer twice and now I'm afraid you're not going to survive this rapid."

But they made it. "It took one and a half hours just to get out of the current to get to shore because we carried so much weight [from the contents of the kitchen boat]. It was an amazing celebration of life."

It was also transformational ". . . to spend your fiftieth birthday with the people you love most in the world and doing something you've never done before, facing death twice, having an adventure. It was life changing. Our friendships will be richer and deeper as a result of this." They had shared something that adults don't normally share. "It was sharing the victory of being alive and it was all so tangible."

Jodi Taylor the outdoorswoman also has an idealistic side. To celebrate fifty, she had commissioned a statue of white marble that is veined in green and originates where she lives, in Marble, Colorado. The piece depicts in abstract form a woman whirling, with hair flung back and arms outstretched.

To name it, she threw a party and asked for suggestions. She chose, appropriately, Iona. Iona is an island off the Scottish coast where ancient Celtics buried their kings because, it was believed, on that island, the veil between heaven and earth is thin.

Her own essence resides in the veil between spirit and reality. Spirituality has been the tuning fork that guides her in teaching leadership. She heads a business called Summit Leadership Solutions Corp. "Learning and creating opportunity for others has been the consistent theme in every job I've ever had. Leadership is the response to make the world a better place for other people."

The marble Iona, now in her home's foyer, expresses that connection, she said, "of leadership, the earth, nurturance, and feminine form."

RON LOGEE AND
MARY ANN JOYCE

*R*on Logee and Mary Ann Joyce headed for the Maine coast from their Virginia home for his birthday. He was depressed, vaguely identifying that he was in "midlife crisis." She, at the same time, was dealing with the amassed possessions left by her father, who had just died.

They needed to talk. They took long walks, taking along in a knapsack, binoculars, camera, and a cassette recorder.

"Whenever we had a profound thought it went right into the recorder, including what we would do after we got back," said Ron. They decided they would take better care of their health, eat carefully, lose weight, and, most important, spend time together. One change they recorded was to get up at the same time in the morning and shower together.

The fiftieth-birthday retreat became a recommitment to each other.

He had served in Vietnam and together they had supported veterans' antiwar activities. Vitally involved in social causes, they have been in a common law marriage since 1973. Yet they had become complacent. ("It was a nice rut, but it was a rut," said Ron.)

"We did more soul searching than usual. We were feeling the pain of getting older." Also, "I was seeing people die up close and seeing what old age is like. The older you get, you pay more attention to your quality of life," said Ron.

> I WANT TO LOOK AT MORE STARS AND SPEND MORE TIME WITH RON.
> —*Mary Ann Joyce*

He was a computer specialist working at home and teaching at a university part-time. As the one who stayed home, shopped, and cooked, he was feeling taken for granted. Then came the juncture. "When you reach your fiftieth, you want to take stock of [your life] and how you want your life to be."

In Maine, he clarified his own issues. "Spending a lot of time in front of a computer isn't that satisfying.

What's fulfilling is to get together with a friend for lunch, going places, seeing things with people you like, looking at the night sky." He redefined his vision: "I want a telescope to look at the night sky. There's a whole universe out there, it's just wonderful." He began to plan going to Europe, exploring out West, and seeing the great parks and canyons.

For Mary Ann, midlife was brought home by confronting what she had hoarded. She had been diagnosed with ovarian cancer and had had a hysterectomy at age thirty-five, a result of the Dalkon Shield IUD, so she knew mortality, but there was more to learn. She had faced the belongings of her father, but "I needed to go through things I've been hoarding and really get down to things I really need." As a librarian, "I always tend to create archives."

She went through her own clothes. "In my own closets, I need to give up some clothes I've been hoarding . . . I was taking stock, separating the wheat from the chaff."

In going through her father's belongings, she decided to take what was important and write a family history to share with siblings, but beyond that, she needed to throw out and let go. She would "strip away the chaff and find the wheat and use it while it's still good—let it sprout instead of letting it disappear in a mass of something."

When she turned the light of these realizations on herself, things became clear. Due to retire in five years, she could hardly wait. Her life would revolve around the commitment made in Maine. "We're unusually close and in tune with each other. No matter what I do at work, no matter how important, the time I spend with Ron is more important whether working or playing together.

"It's a natural part of turning fifty. You begin to look at the rest of your life, how it is finite, and you ask, how do I want to spend it? . . . If you start off with your life mate, it centers you and nothing at work has the same importance.

"I want to look at more stars and spend more time with Ron."

ALAN GOTTLIEB

MAY 2, 1947

With a mysterious rallying cry—
Meraxiroo—Alan Gottlieb's wife and
children pulled off a birthday surprise that took the breath
away from the prominent pro-gun lobbyist and fund-raiser.
And they did it right under his nose.

Tens of thousands of dollars were raised for three of his
personal charities but unknown to him for over a year,
quite a feat. Yet in the end, the story of this public person's
birthday boils down to a private love story. It is a testa-
ment to his wife's love and admiration for her husband.
Julie Gottlieb used a thorough knowledge of his work and
organization and a precise perception of his weaknesses to
pull off the surprise.

"Alan is a very giving, generous person and I knew a

large event was not something he would like," she said. Rather than the big bashes they had both seen, she chose the opposite. "I thought he would, instead of gifts, like to see the money go to charity." So "I decided on three charities that he had an interest in that had nothing to do with his job."

The birthday-invitation package she created set it out plainly. "You know Alan . . . he's never been one to toot his own horn for personal reasons . . . We decided that Alan would like a quiet display of the regard in which he is held."

It continued: "Alan is dedicated to saving individual rights. He has raised millions of dollars to help fund political, social, and charitable causes . . . When it came time to decide what Alan would like as a gift in honor of his birthday, the answer was simple. Your support of one of his personal favorite charities."

She chose the University of Tennessee, Overlake Hospital, and the American Philatelic Foundation, selections that reflect on the affection and humor in their relationship. Their three children were born at Overlake Hospital, the letter continued, the stamp collecting is a

> WHAT HIT ME IS IN THE LAST TWO YEARS, MY FATHER AND MOTHER DIED. I'M THE OLDEST PERSON IN THE FAMILY. I MUST REALLY BE FIFTY.
>
> —Alan Gottlieb

lifetime interest, and the philatelic foundation contributes to school curriculum and physical therapy. Finally, regarding the University of Tennessee: "His wardrobe sports more orange than should be allowed."

With cartoons of orange-garbed bullets decorating the letterhead, the letter concluded, "Given the unending charity of Alan's nature it was simple—another act of kindness."

Julie Gottlieb did not work twenty-plus years as Alan Gottlieb's partner

in direct-mail solicitation and advertising for nothing. She streamlined the logistics. Recipients of the invitation were given materials for two separate mailings. First, a donation card, which they could address to the charity they had chosen. Second, a card to Alan, addressed, however, to Meraxiroo—a conflation of the names of their four children, Amy, Merril, Alexis, and Andrew.

From there, the children took over. For a year, they raided the mailbox at their home/business before their father could get to it. In all, they collected nearly five hundred cards which read: "Happy Birthday, Alan, I sent a contribution in your name to . . . Hope you have many, many more."

At the same time, Julie created a parallel, electronic appeal with a page on the Web site for the Second Amendment Foundation called, "Alan Gottlieb's Fiftieth Birthday." She knew her partner's weakness. Her camouflage was bold, blatant, and flagrant, but "I posted it on our Web site, which I knew he would never visit because I knew at that time he was computer illiterate." Indeed, the appeal was maintained without its founder ever visiting it. However, it was available to nearly one thousand of his colleagues. And they responded.

Julie never doubted she would succeed. "I knew we could do it because we were asking people to donate to charities."

So it came to be that on the night of his birthday, the

chairman of the Citizens Committee for the Right to Keep and Bear Arms, founder of the Second Amendment Foundation, and a director of the American Conservative Union went out for a casual dinner with members of his family and staff, about twelve people altogether. He was presented with a few common gag gifts. Then he received a crystal vase from his family.

In the vase were the cards furtively collected by his children. The honoree, who admits, "I was so busy . . . I didn't even realize I was fifty yet," began to read the cards.

Wonder filled him. "This pile was humongous. I didn't know dinner was on the table. I just wanted to read it all. I was virtually up all night looking at it all.

"All these cards the people turned back, it really touched me. If I could have done it, I would have for myself."

Despite the doing, it was ultimately his wife's admiration that created the gift. Said Julie, "He is a wonderful husband, a superior father, wonderful in-law and uncle, excellent employer, great friend, and very caring human being. I'm still in love with him. This was no less than he deserved. I wish I could've done more."

A Marathon for Krystie

NELDA MERCER

Nineteen ninety-eight began as a disquieting, push-and-pull year for Nelda Mercer, a dietitian and author, even though she had tried to lay a new course for her fifth decade. In the end, her fiftieth was bittersweet. Some issues lay unresolved, but she was able to use her strengths—to meet ambitious goals, train arduously, and go the distance—to serve others.

She had retired from her full-time job, yet returned to it as a consultant. She had suffered from menopausal symptoms and sought treatment, but doctors still needed to calibrate her hormonal therapy. Altogether, the transition to fifty was not clear-cut or comfortable. The past kept pulling her back.

"I was dreading fifty. You start seeing all your little wrinkles."

In response, she willed a turnabout. "I decided I want it positive. I have a great family and wonderful friends; I want to do something that's going to help somebody else."

She befriended a young girl and her parents whom she had observed at church. She knew eleven-year-old Krystie Irwin was ill. "You can tell when they have chemotherapy. I've seen her with hair and without hair."

She reached out to the girl. She knew Krystie had leukemia but "kept my distance until I was thinking about my fiftieth birthday. I always prayed for her and always felt so lucky I had a normal child. I've been really blessed, but I never wanted to get too close because I felt so bad, so bad for her family."

She befriended the family and she told the girl, "I'm going to run this marathon for you." She pledged to run the Honolulu Marathon to raise money for leukemia research.

Yet while she was preparing for her own daughter's high school graduation and entrance to college, and at the same time training for the marathon, Krystie died. In an eleventh-hour effort, Nelda bought expensive, cutting-edge nutritional care for the girl but that failed. "I felt so powerless."

The overachieving firstborn daughter of a Catholic, military family from Texas, Nelda looks back on her life

Sports Graphics Inc.

with regrets and guilts. "I missed out on a lot. I wish I could go back and change but I can't." She wishes she had spent less time away from her daughter. "I had her in day care. I'm not able to have another child. She's my one and only," she says plaintively.

She says she has left the church and yet bemoans that her eighteen-year-old is "too liberal." She started distance running and found she was good at it but begrudges the time it takes.

Yet through her dedication and drive, she became victorious. She had raised five thousand dollars in pledges for Krystie. She donated that money toward Krystie's funeral.

Krystie's death had heightened her gratitude for her own life. For her birthday celebration in the fall of 1998, after Kristie had died, she gave a big dinner in her home. Her invitation read, "My party is to say 'thank you' to my family and many friends for being such a big part of my most fortunate life. I hope you can join me in celebrating my fiftieth birthday." On it she asked for no gifts but donations to the Krystie Irwin Memorial Fund.

"Every year on her birthday, I will make a nice donation to her memorial fund. They lost their only daughter."

She hopes to resolve other issues. As Krystie was dying, she had prayed for a miracle. "I felt a little let down. I feel that God didn't answer my prayer. I don't know what form that answer will come in."

In the meantime, she is able to rely on will and endurance. To help Krystie's mother overcome grief and get back in shape, she offered to teach her what she knows best—tackling long distances. She became her personal trainer. Their goal: the Alaska marathon.

XIII Celebration

"The Grandest Birthday Party Ever"

DEANN BAYLESS

DECEMBER 6, 1948

I think I hear mariachis," she said, and so began a day of music, friends, and food that for Deann Bayless became the celebration of a lifetime and the highest expression of love from her husband.

"Let's go and see," he said. And so Rick Bayless, restaurateur and chef, led his wife and partner in the two premier Mexican restaurants of the country out their front door that Sunday morning.

On the sidewalk, nine blue and silver–clad mariachi players were strolling toward them, singing *"Las Mañanitas,"* the Mexican birthday song. Behind them walked some thirty friends and family, all singing. At the head of the procession walked Lanie, their seven-year-old daughter, carrying a package wrapped in lush-green banana leaf.

As if seven years old herself, Deann clapped her hands over her mouth. She wept. She opened Lanie's package to find two leis of densely woven orchids, one for Rick and one for her. They had been ordered from Thailand, where the family had spent a magical vacation six weeks earlier.

Rick invited all into the house for a breakfast of pozole (a traditional Mexican soup) and mescal (a cactus liquor) and after an hour of song and spontaneous dance, he announced that the group should board the bus. "The what?" said Deann, making her most succinct and articulate pronouncement of the day. She would more often express herself with floods of happy tears and speechless wonder as the day unfolded.

The friends, local as well as those who flew into Chicago from Mexico, Seattle, New York, and elsewhere, boarded a bus that made surprise stops (for Deann) in an itinerary of music and food that none would ever forget.

One of them, sixty-three-year-old Bob Hoogstoel, wrote about the birthday in a ten-page, single-space letter when he returned home. He sent it to lift up the spirits of a friend in Florida whose husband of sixty years was dying of cancer. He titled it, "The Grandest Birthday Party Ever."

The bus stopped first at the House of Blues, a venue whose every inside inch is plastered with outsider art, a "funky opera house" to Bob. Rick had reserved the third balcony for the birthday group. As they listened to a rousing, stomping performance by a gospel choir, guests served themselves brunch from a buffet.

Following that, all adjourned to a nearby high-rise apartment where the Bayless restaurants' chef lived on the fifty-sixth floor. The group toasted Deann with champagne in engraved glasses while Deann cut into two stunning cakes festooned in spun-sugar flowers and smooth chocolate tiles. In this intimate interim, friends toasted, read to, and reminisced with Deann.

The words were heartfelt and original. A sixteen-year-old boy stood to read a poem he had composed to her, others recounted histories of their friendship with Deann, stating their admiration for her and Rick. Rick read to her the sonnet, "Love, how often I loved you without seeing" by poet Pablo Neruda.

Then the announcement was made, once more, to board the bus. Deann, wordless, followed.

The bus wound its way to a church where the maître d' of the Baylesses' restaurants, who is also a musician, conducted the choir in a program of choral and organ music. It was a powerful moment in a day whose theme had been music. Deann, who was tearing up less frequently, acknowledged this gracefully. Sacred music was an integral part of her Dutch Reform Church tradition, and singing was at the heart of her upbringing, she said.

Come early evening, the bus headed homeward. Home, however, had been transformed in the six hours since they departed into a tropical paradise, a scene from the flower markets in Thailand. Orchids, orchids, and more orchids were amassed around hundreds of candles. Even Deann's bathroom was transformed into a floral fantasy—the Jacuzzi was being drawn, candles were lit, and Deann was invited to immerse herself in the scented bathwater.

"Can I be wife number two?" asked one friend.

Soon, a swing dance band was warming up (for the "party" Deann had expected) and the first of more than 100 additional guests arrived, including their restaurant employees. Many said they owe to Deann thanks for being the glue of the restaurant, a mother to the community. The caterers, who had transformed the home into the tropical paradise and tony club, began serving superb Southeast Asian food.

There were no superlatives left. The day had infused Deann's friends with similar emotions—many had shed tears and felt forever transformed. Toni Sobel of Oaxaca, Mexico, appreciated the scale of the event—"How many husbands spend a year organizing a celebration for their wives?"—but also its intangible import. As a result of the party, she said, she now reaches out more to people, draws closer to her own religion, and rethinks her purpose: "I wonder just what I am going to do with the years left to me [she is fifty-four]."

For the friends who had come from afar, other celebratory events bracketed the Sunday party. There was a surprise dinner at the Baylesses' upscale restaurant the previous night. The day following the party ended with all cooking

DAY OF DEANN GROEN BAYLESS
50TH BIRTHDAY PARTY

9:45AM Guests & Mariachis arrive in the church parking lot located on the other (North) side of elevated train track next to R & D's house. See map.
Out-of-towners—take taxi to 1758 N. Hermitage and look for us. There you will meet Jen Fite with leis to give to Deann

10:00 We begin our walk to the house and sing the Mexican birthday son (las Mañanitas) when Deann answers the door. Pozole and mescal are waiting for us!

11:30 A bus arrives to take us to the House of Blues We will all enjoy a gospel brunch in the private balcony; Mimosas to celebrate!

2pm Brunch is over and we are off to the apartment of Geno Bahena (sous chef at Frontera Grill) located in the same building as House of Blues.
Champagne will be waiting for us to make our birthday toasts to Deann. Please bring a special poem, thought, story or special wish to share with Deann and the group for her birthday.

3:15pm Bus is waiting to take us to St. Paul's United Church of Christ

FRONTERA FOODS, INC.
VOICE • 312.595.1624
FAX • 312.595.1625

445 NORTH CLARK STREET
SUITE #205
CHICAGO, ILLINOIS 60610

FRONTERA GRILL • TOPOLOBAMPO
VOICE • 312.661.1434
FAX • 312.661.1830

at home with the Baylesses. Bob Hoogstoel wrote on page ten of his letter: "As we approached the end of the meal I began having those awful pangs I get when I know something wonderful is ending."

Words would come to Deann in the months following her birthday. Even then, she could only say that she had not yet absorbed its significance, except to restate what she learned about receiving—that what she took in would flow out again in a complete circle of giving and receiving.

As a professional organizer of entertainments and tours, as one who works behind the scenes in hospitality, she was still overwhelmed. "There was something about its bigness. It was so totally filling. If I never had another party in my life, I'm fine. I'm the luckiest person I know.

"It was so incredibly over the top. It left me so full I can't imagine not being full of love after that," she said. She felt as she had at her wedding, that those she loved most were present at the most important moment of her life. This, however, was for her alone. "I'm used to being in the background [behind Rick]. To put me in the foreground in such a big way, it was a huge gift of love."

Rick could only hope for such a response to the party—the creation of a "magical moment when you're able to move into a different dimension of existence." There are extravagant, rich people's parties that never reach "that sense of communion," he said. "My goal for this party was to be able to achieve that sort of transcendence." He cites Mexican culture for teaching him the fiesta, for which the poor will pour their resources, love, joy, creativity, and energy into a gathering that binds all participants at a soulful level.

Deann's day was soulful from beginning to end. But for her, there was one single soaring moment—when Rick read the love sonnet. "The day revolved around that moment. It was a public affirmation of his love, something I always dreamed of hearing. And I got it."

JAN STEINMARK

DECEMBER 5, 1947

From the time in her twenties when she re-created her name—a conflation of hers and her then-husband's names—Jan Steinmark has continued to jam together all she gathers, live by her own terms, and fashion her own inimitable style.

Her blazing blue house with the jonquil-colored shutters and red flowers in the window boxes throngs with a mosaic of collectibles. Among the knickknacks are shelf after shelf of Santas, snowmen, and King Arthur memorabilia.

On the walls, two posters that express her joie de vivre elbow for space. One is titled "Dancers of the Third Age"— a string of gleeful stompers expressing wild yearnings. "There's a shorter lady in there that I identify with," she says, brown eyes twinkling in the same five-foot-two-inch frame of the once mischievous college student.

The other is a snow-haired, wrinkled Grandma Moses gazing out over her fulsome, long-lived breasts. She is flexing her biceps and thrusting out the bulky bust; it is studded with some forty buttons. Among the chestful of messages are: Seeker of Truth, Fat Pride, Protect Human Rights, Hug a Teacher, and Bread Not Bombs. The title of the poster is "Her Strength Is in Her Principles."

"I want to be like her when I grow up," says Jan.

This child-woman celebrated fifty as a child-woman would, with unabashed delight. She held a slumber party. The party turned out to be a reunion of special education teachers from her past and present. She held it in the large basement of a coworker's house. Husbands were told they weren't allowed, although the hostess's husband was to stay close in case extra pizza was needed.

FIFTY WASN'T DEPRESSING FOR ME. IT WAS EXCITING. I JUST LIKED BEING ALIVE.

—Jan Steinmark

She and the coworkers had discussed the sleepover for years. "My assistants were concerned about getting older; they were always checking for wrinkles and gray hair. I was never hung up on this age thing. For me, each year is something to celebrate. I always had birthdays and celebrated them. Fifty wasn't depressing for me. It was exciting. I just liked being alive."

Her younger cohorts' obsession challenged her to think through her attitude; a lightbulb pinged on. She was clearer than ever about why there was a need to celebrate. It even happens at a funeral. "When we die we want people to cry a lot, and we want to have a good time and then we celebrate. So why not at fifty?"

Twenty-seven women showed up, and seven lasted the duration. Those who stayed were asleep by one A.M. and all cleared out by ten the next morning. No surprise, those who slept on the floor felt achy.

Still, "we had the best time, catching up." Special ed teachers have a special bond because "if you don't bond you go crazy."

Jan had had her epiphany on her twenty-ninth birthday and never looked back. "I went in a closet and cried and cried." It was a few years after her divorce and before she decided to have a child on her own. Since that time and especially since she had Eric,

> IT'S BEEN A REAL YEAR OF CHANGE. I'VE PROBABLY GONE THROUGH MORE CHANGES THAN I DID AS A TEENAGER.
>
> —Jan Steinmark

now in college, she has continued to re-create herself and to live her idealism. "I'm more realistic with my idealism, but still plugging away at it. I'm not expecting overnight changes."

She has changed careers steadily, from teaching moderately handicapped children to providing resources for the blind, to assisting minority students, to working with cancer patients, to working with crippled children, to teaching mentally handicapped adults. Each has been a moulting stage for the next: "I loved each job. And when they're over, they're over."

Now she looks forward to retiring so she can actively support gay and lesbian causes. She is not lesbian but it is important for heterosexuals to support the cause to emphasize that it is a human rights issue. She influences seven to ten students as a special ed teacher, but as a supporter of gay and lesbian civil rights, she can affect hundreds.

Although some of her friends have suffered through the empty nest syndrome, she has not. "I'm alone and I'm not lonely and I'm my own best friend." She raised her son as she has lived. "I definitely traveled to the beat of my own drum and I raised Eric to be that way too."

Being single is a gift. "I don't think I would have been

the same person if I had stayed married. I don't think I would've had the freedom to be what I've become. I don't think I would have felt as free."

As the "Her Strength Is in Her Principles" poster suggests, there is power in liking yourself as you are. "I'm content with what I am and I want that to continue and I want to stay involved."

Mountaintop Wedding

ANTONIA ALLEGRA

FEBRUARY 21, 1946

At ten I was a kid, at twenty I was married with one kid, at thirty I was a working mom with three kids, at forty I was divorced with three kids. At fifty the kids are all on their own and I'm totally free. And by circumstance, I'm getting married." So Toni Allegra summed up her life and the exclamation point that her fiftieth birthday added.

She had been swept by the joy of turning fifty, and she threw a day-long party. The name of the party was "Joie de Vivre."

The following morning, a "perfectly beautiful, clear day," she and her husband-to-be, along with their children (three each), headed up to the peak of Mount St. Helena, the highest point in Napa Valley, California. There, on the craggy rocks that overlook the full sweep from the Pacific Ocean to Nevada, they said their vows.

Joie de vivre was the theme of her birthday party before she knew she was getting married. The writer, editor, and creator of happenings in the region, a self-employed woman whom many have dubbed a "launcher," was embracing fifty and feeling great about it.

She had rented a barn, created an invitation (they were already in the laser printer), and had made a guest list of 150 when the completely unexpected marriage proposal came. "My plan and whole object was to introduce my friends to my other friends and that was the best birthday present I could imagine," she said.

She had been "absolutely stars-in-the-sky in love" but at the same time she had also been "solo for fourteen years," so she did not dream of marriage. She needed time to think.

In the meantime the plans for the birthday were moving ahead. By the time she decided to say yes, the only day on which the two could gather their families was to be the day of her birthday party.

With the rhythm-and-blues band wailing that night, the two gathered their children in front of the guests. She approached the microphone and broke the news. "We announced that the next day we would be going to the top of the mountain for a family wedding. All the kids and Donn and I introduced ourselves to this loving group of best friends. It was an incredible situation."

The woman who describes herself as "a communitarian," for her love of people and for belonging to so many groups, gave her friends something to celebrate. "And the place just went crazy. Everybody was laughing and dancing."

CINDY HINDS AND
LESLIE WEISS
AUGUST 1, 1947, AND FEBRUARY 26, 1947

*C*indy Hinds and Leslie Weiss had stolen moments between business trips and their children's schedules to keep up their college friendship. In the crazy patchwork of mobile career woman and static mom, they stayed in touch by sneaking in a joint meal here and there. Luckily, they each traveled occasionally to the other's city for conventions and meetings.

Rather than let luck continue to dole out favors, however, the two seized opportunity. "We had never before spent time together other than as ships in the night," said Leslie. "At breakfast we said, 'We just can't do this.' We are at a time in life where we need to spend time together—the friendship is too special. We now have the moment, let's seize it." Sure enough, they did. A few months later, they were in Vermont for a one-week horseback trek, going from New England inn to New England inn, their fiftieth-birthday present to each other and themselves. In addition, they made a commitment to do something together annually.

"Fifty is about an opportunity," said Leslie.

The idea formed when Cindy was driving Leslie to the Denver airport. Talk turned to how Leslie's son was in college and Cindy's daughter was a teenager; how the parents of each were relatively well. They proclaimed the obvious and asked only one question. "Hey we don't have the obstacles anymore. We have money, we employ ourselves, and our children are grown. Let's go have fun together and do it each year. Why not?" said Leslie.

> ENOUGH OF THIS SLAVE LABOR AND DO-GOODING. I NEED TO HAVE FUN. I'VE PAID MY DUES. I'LL ALWAYS WORK WITH THE DOWNTRODDEN AND THE POOR. THERE'S JUST OTHER THINGS TO DO. FIFTY IS ABOUT AN OPPORTUNITY.
>
> —Leslie Weiss

It was, by her account, "a moment of glee."

The two, college roommates and best friends, members at each other's wedding, and supporters for key crises in the other's life, found during their get-together that, indeed,

"We can pick up where we left off. It's just seamless," said Leslie.

Cindy had her own epiphany earlier. She was filling out her résumé and was startled by its reflection. "This is pretty boring—who cares I've done all these things related to work." She slowly inched work toward home and began spending more time with her daughter. When she compared her generation's menopause to that of her mother's, and noted her daughter's growing independence, she concluded, "If I don't find things to do that are beyond work, I'm going to be an unhappy person."

She hired a trainer and she bought a horse. "It was the beginning of saying there are other things to do besides work. The whole horse thing was so symbolic for me." Riding had been a childhood passion.

She then planned a year of sustained celebration—a family reunion, a trip to Santa Fe for the summer opera season, and the culmination, a week-long retreat with Leslie.

Although they picked up the friendship in seamless fashion, they found qualitative differences in the relationship as midlifers, some of it enriching. "It feels more settled. Neither one of us is so new and green at life that we're in a constant panic. We've been through different transitions. [But] we really have shared so many things. We've just lived through a lot together," said Leslie.

Since that fiftieth-year horseback trail, they have gone to Wales and are planning adventure trips to Spain and Portugal.

"There's no time for apologizing. We're at an age where we don't have forever. Let's not waste it. Life is really precious and there's lots of ways of responding to it that's not

in work and not in child care. And some of it is getting to know the world, so let's go have adventures.

"I want to go to places that take physical energy sooner. But I still expect to be riding horseback at eighty-five," said Leslie.

XIV Millennium

DAVE JOHNSTON

NOVEMBER 7, 1950

ave Johnston takes the symbol of turning fifty at the millennium seriously and he thinks all who are in his generation should hear it as a clarion call.

The so-called Y2K bug is a mere wake-up call. "Environmental situations—global warming, ozone and oil depletion, among others—will hit us across the face." Compared to them, "Y2K is a blip in the map."

The building consultant and student of Buckminster Fuller has given his intelligence, career, and energies to sustainable living.

"We're outstripping the carrying capacity of the Earth. We can't feed, house, support, or clean up after the number of people we have." The population of the Earth is six billion currently and will double by approximately 2025, he said. "The only way we can make it through the next quarter century is for those of us who are aware of our current lifestyle to assume leadership positions and provide alternatives at a very rapid rate."

This "intelligent response" is needed from him and those in his generation. "At the last antinuclear demonstration I attended in 1974, I came away committed to providing alternatives and not just being against something." The question he posed then: "If we were going to shut down the nukes, then what?"

In the interim twenty-five years, he has dedicated himself to "looking at systems," seeing if they work, and learning alternatives, he said. His clarion call constitutes his celebration.

There is hope. "We know how to do things better and it's time to do what we know how to do."

There is joy. "There's joy in making the commitment to be more self-reliant and less dependent." That joy is "similar to the joy a mother feels when she snatches her baby out of the clutches of a wild animal. There's joy in acting on my beliefs in a concrete, tangible way. I'm leading by example how we enter the next millennium."

Even before he turned fifty, he gathered a group "to welcome in the millennium and to put forth a declaration of sustainable, harmonious living within the planet." His book *Building Green in a Black and White World* (Home Builders Press) was released in January 2000. "We want to create a road map for the politicians, corporations, and nonprofits to help implement a sustainable future."

His personal declaration reads, "I intend for my fiftieth to be a celebration of a set of values for the twenty-first century. I will welcome all to join me in embracing the future with optimism. The values include the following:

1. I will have a net positive impact on my environment both socially and ecologically every day.

2. I will reduce my consumption of processed products and buy closer to the source.

3. I will reduce my personal dependence on and use of petro-fuels by converting as fully as possible to our only income source of energy, solar.

4. I will work to reinvent a more appropriate transport vehicle that conveniently moves people and material with much less petro-fuel required.

5. I will conduct myself with due diligence to preserving the delicate balance of the planet's rain forest resource.

6. I will continue to catalyze the construction industry to build greener and more environmentally appropriate buildings around the world.

7. I will assist anyone who is interested in creating more sustainable lifestyles by providing information, education, and products to facilitate the process.

8. I will participate in the local initiatives to create a more sustainable local community.

9. I will support only the government leaders, on all levels, who commit to designing the future with intention rather than status quo.

10. I will follow spirit to live a harmonious life with all living things."

XV Sunset

Angkor Wat and the Cycle of Life

JANE ALT

MAY 26, 1951

As she nears fifty, Jane Alt feels the pull of death and of what is beyond. She can think of two experiences that would give meaning to the year.

The first is a near-death experience. Knowing that might be difficult, she would substitute a return to Angkor Wat in Cambodia. "There's a part of me that just wants to go to a place that's quiet and commune with the greater forces." An established psychotherapist and a rising photographic talent, she finds herself personally and artistically drawn to what is beyond words and beyond reality.

In her lifetime she has witnessed plenty of beautiful moments. At twenty-one, she looked out a port window and watched a beautiful sunrise while sailing from Italy to

Crete. Much as she has wanted to recapture that beauty, she now no longer desires it. At the approach to fifty, she hungers for a deeper force. "Angkor Wat has been there for centuries, it has outlived many people."

Angkor Wat extends a personal exploration of solitude and spirituality. "I've been doing a lot with tai chi [the Chinese, slow-movement exercise] lately, trying to develop the more spiritual side of myself."

A return to this mystical center would also complete a personal cycle. Her husband, children, and she had witnessed a sunset there while vacationing in Vietnam and Cambodia years earlier. The monks had finished chanting evensong and dusk was falling as they left the temple. The trip from the temple to their hotel vibrated with intensity. With every pore tuned to a possible ambush by robbers or hijackers, her husband felt his every instinct rise to a high pitch. The guide, likewise, hurriedly herded them, his eyes darting furtively.

Meanwhile, her instincts rose to a different dimension—to a serenity she could almost touch. It was saturated by the setting sun and the sound of chant ringing clear in the opaque dusk. For her the moment was powerfully hushed and holy. "There's something about daybreak and dusk, the transition. With my art that's what I'm interested in. It's like birth and death."

She is predisposed to such questions because "it's a life journey. If you're inclined to asking the questions, they start revealing themselves. Everyone goes through raising a family, having a career, and you kind of wonder what the purpose is. I think there's just a continuum of life that pre-dates me and exists after I'm gone. And I suppose thinking of Angkor Wat and being there is one way of tapping into that."

Birth and death have captured her focus as an artist, especially death. "My parents are aging and I'm aging. It's the fall of our lives. I'm trying to figure out what it all means."

The search leads her to life cycles and infinity. She has searched intently. To study birth, she has photographed two home deliveries and found in them parallels to nature's life cycles. There was "the image when the baby was starting to crown. The circular form of the perineum was very dark. And out of the darkness comes lightness— the baby's head—almost like a flower. It reminds me of how nature's forms repeat themselves throughout life. It seemed very ordinary." At another birth, she was struck by the juxtaposition of extraordinary and ordinary. "It was really glorious. The baby is in such a pure state. It was really a thrill and I feel I can watch him grow up. But it's not that different from watching an amaryllis bulb shoot up and start to die."

Her studies of death nearly always juxtapose it to new life. Her black-and-white compositions catch the transition between them, in ethereal shades of gray. For example, she created one shot of a dead dog surrounded by fallen leaves through which new shoots sprout, and another, of a girl's white dress frozen in ice with leaves strewn about.

> I THINK WE COME FROM NOTHINGNESS AND GO BACK TO NOTHINGNESS.
>
> —Jane Alt

She volunteered at an AIDS clinic so as to become intimate with death. Inexorably she was drawing the conclusion that death was ordinary, as ordinary as birth. It was also as miraculous, as beautiful, as natural, and as cyclical.

"I used to hate it that fall comes and leaves would drop. But two years ago I realized that the trees and the branches were so beautiful. Even as the leaves fall off, there's beauty to that."

She turns the lens on herself. "I could see the beauty in

my gray hair. I dyed my hair for a few years, then I stopped. I said to myself, I've earned them. My body has more character than it had in my twenties. There are the wrinkles and sags. I've had children. My body shows the signs that I've lived."

Her parents might fear death but, "I'm not afraid of death. I think it's going to be this release. There's going to be just a relief, total peace . . . again. I think we come from nothingness and go back to nothingness. That's what I'm trying to figure out. I think the answers are in nature and I think things come and go and I'm trying to live in the present as much as possible."

She had witnessed dusk at Angkor Wat and now she would bring her presence and her eye to sunrise at the temple—to beginnings, to the sacred, and to the infinite. Birth to death, sunrise to sunset. "It's trying to be with something that's greater than one life."

And that "intensifies my sense of living."

Dusk, Angkor Wat.

Ideas for Fiftieth Celebrations

Have a slumber party. Work around the theme of "comfort" (or "chocolate" as it turns out for many women).

Instead of purchased gifts ask for:
- ♦ something made by the giver
- ♦ a memento of the past
- ♦ a reading or a poem

Reconnect. Create a year-long project in which you reconnect with friends, mentors, and family. For example:
- ♦ write letters to those who mattered to you most
- ♦ locate and call friends from grade school, high school, and college
- ♦ revisit places in which you have lived

- ◆ revisit those with whom you have lost the thread
- ◆ revisit older relatives and friends

Recognize mother. Send flowers to the one person who regards your birth and the date as the central celebration of her life. Begin a tradition of sending flowers to your mother on your birthday.

Reunite family. If you are part of a large family or large extended family, you may want to organize, or start, family reunions around the siblings' fiftieth birthdays as a celebration. This works especially well if you come from a large family.

Organize a fiftieth birthday for close friends within high school and college reunions. You may want to commit to meeting with the same group annually.

Start a secret greeting card campaign, ask that they be sent to a separate address, and give them altogether to the honoree.

Organize donations to the honoree's favorite charity.

Celebrate with a sentimental dinner at a restaurant of the '60s or '70s, with nostalgic menu items.

At a party for several fifty-year-olds, create posters of each celebrant using photos of the '70s. Ask guests to guess which poster identifies which celebrant.

Some Famous Fifty-Year-Olds

1946

Candace Bergen
Cher
Connie Chung
Bill Clinton
Larry Csonka
Sally Field
Cynthia Gregory
Greg Gumbel
Gregory Hines
Reggie Jackson
Diane Keaton
Barry Manilow
Peter Martins
Liza Minnelli
Tricia Nixon

Dolly Parton
Robert B. Reich
Susan Sarandon
Pete Singer
Sylvester Stallone
Shelby Steele
Donald Trump
Ben Vereen
Bob Vila
Diane von Furstenberg
Lesley Ann Warren
André Watts
Christine Todd Whitman
Judy Woodruff

1947

Kareem Abdul-Jabbar
Dave Barry
Johnny Bench
David Bowie
Henry Cisneros
Hillary Rodham Clinton
Glenn Close
Billy Crystal
David Eisenhower
Danny Glover
Arlo Guthrie
Elton John
Luci Baines Johnson
Stephen King
David Letterman

Carol Moseley-Braun
Edward James Olmos
Jim Plunkett
Faith Popcorn
Dan Quayle
Salman Rushdie
Nolan Ryan
Arnold Schwarzenegger
Peter Serkin
Frank Shorter
O. J. Simpson
Steven Spielberg
Danielle Steel
Cheryl Tiegs

1948

Mikhail Baryshnikov
Kathy Bates
Ben Chavis
Alice Cooper
Dave Cowens
Julie Eisenhower
Peggy Fleming
Albert Gore Jr.
Tipper Gore

Bryant Gumbel
Jeremy Irons
Donna Karan
Barbara Mandrell
Richard Simmons
James Taylor
Clarence Thomas
Andrew Lloyd Webber

1949

George Foreman
Phyllis George
Richard Gere
Whoopi Goldberg
William Randolph
    Hearst III
Bruce Jenner
Jamaica Kincaid
Annie Leibovitz
Diana Nyad
Paloma Picasso

Wolfgang Puck
Marilyn Quayle
Ahmad Rashad
Lionel Richie
Sissy Spacek
Bruce Springsteen
Meryl Streep
Ivana Trump
Scott Turow
Twiggy

1950

Natalie Cole
Julius Erving
Morgan Fairchild
Gennifer Flowers
Henry Louis Gates Jr.
Lani Guinier
Arianna Huffington
William Hurt
Lance Ito
Bianca Jagger

Shelley Long
Joan Lunden
Bobby McFerrin
Bill Murray
Peggy Noonan
Jane Pauley
Cybill Shepherd
Wendy Wasserstein
Stevie Wonder

MY STORY

During the year that I was collecting fiftieth-birthday stories, I was often asked if I would include my own. I answered firmly that this was not a book about me; its genesis was never egocentric. Besides, at forty-nine, I had no idea whether or how to celebrate the looming fifty.

As the year progressed and I became intimate with the subjects of the book, I saw more transparently the gratitude, joy, compassion, generosity, humility, strengths, and frailties of each individual. With each interview and meeting, I was touched and moved. Certain as I was that I would find that these "ordinary" people, not the rich and famous, used all the fruits of the imagination and love to create their own celebrations—and I did—I was stumped about my own. How could I match them? How could I not imitate them?

There seemed no reason to celebrate. I was jobless, a single parent, and working in isolation on a long-shot project, this book. In an earlier fit of austerity and a show of strength, I stopped coloring my gray hair, but otherwise, I could cite no markers and no achievements. I had let go of my career, was starting to freelance, and was raising a fifteen-year-old. My nose was to the grindstone. I had been on my own for ten years and by gritting my teeth I would finish child-rearing. My task was to hold on, not change, and certainly not to celebrate.

Then, gifts and opportunities rained on me. They were like the night sky's stars to which I finally gave time to twinkle. Once I saw them, I no longer had reason not to fly to them. A high school friend sent me a ticket to Paris to meet her there; another in Germany sent me a rail ticket to go to her home. For the first time in my working, single life, I had the time and space to accept. My son was old enough to withstand a short absence (he was overjoyed). Later that year, friends invited me to travel to Thailand, where I grew up. The trip reconnected me to my roots. Having time and space mirrored a timeless and spacious quality shaping within me. Rather than demur, I was able to receive these gifts as expressions of lifelong caring with deep, growing gratitude.

Somehow, having released so much, I felt for the first time since the birth of my child that I was capable of fully receiving and giving.

Then, unexpectedly, I fell in love. Out of this grew an even more expansive feeling, and it was in this state that, when I sat down to write my Christmas letter, I could create out of it a celebration. It would be with words, it would integrate all I had lived and express my faith in transformation. It would be a telling of my story—a story about dreams coming true and allowing them to happen—in a way everybody's story.

I had intended to take the pressure off my son and friends for a party with my letter. All the same, in January of 1999, two of them threw me a magical, tulip-showered dinner, something I had dared not hope for. It was an affair for twenty which soared with moments of song. And, at the end of that year, my book, this book, which I had dreamed of, was published.

Here is what I wrote (accompanied by a photo greeting card).

a narrative for the longest night . . .

A father sent his daughter across the Pacific Ocean many years ago to Mei Guo, The Beautiful Country. He put into her hand a bundle of green, tight, uniform bills. This is Beautiful Country money, he said, to keep you.

Eye-water coursed down her mother's face as the sixteen-year-old climbed into a winged ship. When it tore off the ground, it seemed to rip the very roots of her soul. She wept. And the rain in her being joined the storm that pelted the ship as it flew. She grieved until no more food and water spilled from her and she was empty.

Even as part of her had died, the metal ship skirted the typhoon and found haven.

While she waited to continue the fractured journey, she wandered the graceless halls of a foreign port and she saw, among jumbled newspaper stands, a picture that lit her darkened soul and stirred some distant song. The picture bore mischief. Its image had eyes that danced and spoke of fearless love. She took out the bundle of tight, green, uniform bills to pay for it. She carried it with her to Beautiful Country.

The image of the mischievous dog accompanied her everywhere. It was taped to dorm rooms, in attic and basement apartments. Each year, she unrolled it from a stash of dusty posters.

The corners frayed; the top edge wore thin with masking tape. When she married, she slapped school glue on its back, stuck it to a board and framed it. Often, as she lived and grew in the country that was at once beautiful and ugly, and her life was visited by pain and joy, she neglected it. But after her divorce, she hung it again in the small house she found for herself and her son.

One spring, the mother and son brought home a puppy that had been given up for adoption. She didn't want it, but the boy insisted. On the morning she was sure she would return the unruly puppy, she turned to stare at the picture hanging above the old brown couch. She looked into its dancing eyes. It

My 1999 greeting card.

was as if the image had leapt out of the frame and into life. She kept the puppy.

One day, although it was disallowed, the dog leapt onto the old brown couch (encouraged by the unruly boy). It curled up. It slept as if it belonged there. Under the picture she bought long ago, his eyes opened and invited her to dance . . .

The heartsong that stirred so many years ago in her deepest grief finally gave voice. The woman now lives in gratitude, wholing herself, trusting dim dreams and mysteries, listening for distant songs and healing. This coming year, she will be fifty.